AT THE NAME OF JESUS

AT
THE NAME
OF
JESUS

Sarah Hornsby

Chosen Books
A Division of Baker Book House
Grand Rapids, Michigan 49506

Scripture references used in this edition unless marked
KJV (The King James Version) are taken from the New
American Standard version of the Holy Bible used with
permission of The Lockman Foundation, LaHabra, Cali-
fornia, copyright © 1960, 1962, 1963, 1968, 1971, 1972,
1973, 1975.

Library of Congress Cataloging in Publication Data
Hornsby, Sarah.
    At the Name of Jesus.

    1. Jesus Christ—Prayer books and devotions—
English.   2. Devotional calendars.   I. Title.
BT306.5.H67   1984   232   83-26245
ISBN 0-8007-9078-2

A Chosen Book
Copyright © 1983 by Sarah Hornsby
Chosen Books are published by Fleming H. Revell
a division of Baker Book House Company
P.O. Box 6287, Grand Rapids, MI 49516-6287

Fifteenth printing, January 1993

Printed in the United States of America

A special thanks to the women in the
Cullowhee Presbyterian Church prayer
group for inspiration and encouragement,
to Gayle Woody and Kathy Cottrell, my
friends in the Lord Jesus who wrote some
of the pages, and to Diane Collins who
helped proofread.

Some Ideas on How to Use
At the Name of Jesus

Each day in a quiet time you can:

1. Praise God for Jesus. Praise Him for the specific quality in Jesus described for that day. Ask Him to help you worship in Spirit and in truth. Let your mind focus on His greatness, His glory.

2. As you praise, read the Scripture at the bottom of the page. Ask Jesus to speak to you. This would be a word of edification, exhortation, and consolation from God specifically to you. Take time to listen and write down what you hear. You will be amazed at the wisdom He gives you for your circumstances when you reread these words.

3. Pray for the government, for yourself, and others in this name of Jesus. He has promised that His power is available to us. On the page for the day, briefly write your request and ask God to show you a Scripture which is His will for the situation. Later when you read over these requests, place a check or the date the prayer was answered.

4. Read back over the previous days' Names, Scriptures and praises to get a cumulative effect as you begin praising Him on a new day. This is particularly helpful when you feel tired or discouraged.

5. Share the Name of Jesus and Scripture with your friends and loved ones on their birthdays.

6. Share the insights you have received with someone else as an encouragement to them.

O Come Let Us Adore Him!

JESUS is the
ALPHA, the first letter in the Greek
alphabet. Jesus speaks to my heart and
says . . . Before anything was made, I
was with God and the Holy Spirit. For
Me and with Me and by Me all things
were created, visible and invisible. In Me
all things hold together—the universe,
your world, all the nations, your family,
health, and life. Put them in My hand so
that I can work My way in you . . .

"I am the Alpha and the Omega, the first and the
last, the beginning and the end."

REVELATION 22:13

JESUS is the
APOSTLE. He is the One God sent,
His ambassador. I hear Jesus saying . . .
I came to you, died on a cross for you,
was raised for you, and now I come to
you. God wants you for His own, so I
keep coming, keep loving you. I want to
claim the country of your heart for the
true and living God. I want to establish
My government in you . . .

"Therefore, holy brethren, partakers of a heavenly
calling, consider Jesus, the Apostle and High
Priest of our confession."

HEBREWS 3:1

JESUS is the
ALMIGHTY. He has absolute power over all. As I ask God to speak to me, I hear Him say . . . All power has been given to Jesus in heaven and in earth. Let Him establish His power in you today. Let Him take every fear and burden of your life. He is able to do great things in you, for you, and through you, today . . .

"And He put all things in subjection under His feet, and gave Him as head over all things to the church, which is His body."

EPHESIANS 1:20ff.

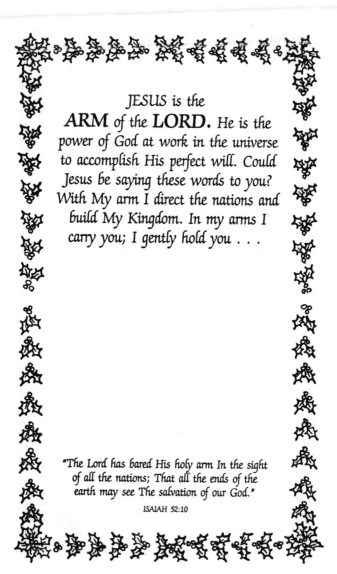

JESUS is the
ARM of the **LORD.** He is the
power of God at work in the universe
to accomplish His perfect will. Could
Jesus be saying these words to you?
With My arm I direct the nations and
build My Kingdom. In my arms I
carry you; I gently hold you . . .

"The Lord has bared His holy arm In the sight
of all the nations; That all the ends of the
earth may see The salvation of our God."

ISAIAH 52:10

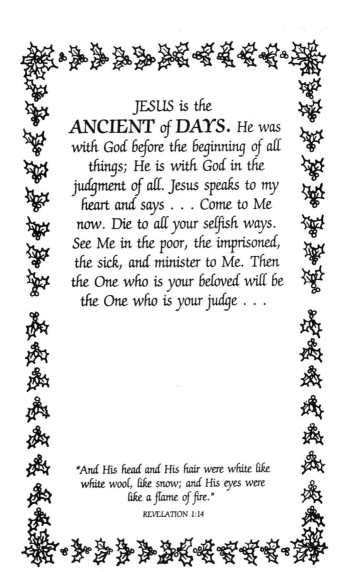

JESUS is the
ANCIENT of **DAYS.** He was
with God before the beginning of all
things; He is with God in the
judgment of all. Jesus speaks to my
heart and says . . . Come to Me
now. Die to all your selfish ways.
See Me in the poor, the imprisoned,
the sick, and minister to Me. Then
the One who is your beloved will be
the One who is your judge . . .

"And His head and His hair were white like
white wool, like snow; and His eyes were
like a flame of fire."

REVELATION 1:14

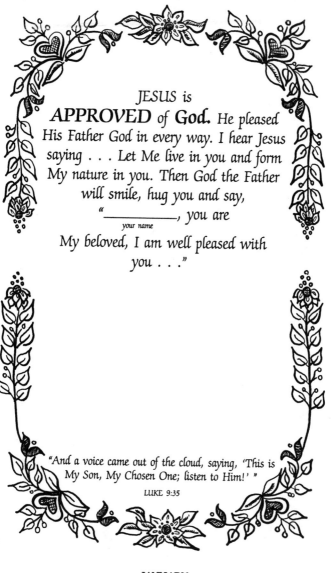

JESUS is **APPROVED** of **God.** He pleased His Father God in every way. I hear Jesus saying . . . Let Me live in you and form My nature in you. Then God the Father will smile, hug you and say, "_____, you are
_{your name}
My beloved, I am well pleased with you . . ."

"And a voice came out of the cloud, saying, 'This is My Son, My Chosen One; listen to Him!' "

LUKE 9:35

JESUS is the

ARK. When we enter into His life, no storm can harm us. Jesus says to my heart . . . Come into Me and bring your loved ones. I care about the safety of your family more than you do. I am the One who will protect and keep them through the storms of life . . .

"By faith Noah, being warned by God about things not yet seen, in reverence prepared an ark for the salvation of his household."

HEBREWS 11:7

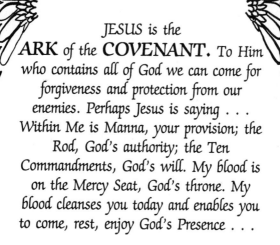

JESUS is the
ARK of the **COVENANT.** To Him
who contains all of God we can come for
forgiveness and protection from our
enemies. Perhaps Jesus is saying . . .
Within Me is Manna, your provision; the
Rod, God's authority; the Ten
Commandments, God's will. My blood is
on the Mercy Seat, God's throne. My
blood cleanses you today and enables you
to come, rest, enjoy God's Presence . . .

" . . . the Holy of Holies . . . and the ark of the
covenant covered on all sides with gold, in which
was a golden jar holding the manna, and
Aaron's rod which budded, and the tables of
the covenant. And above it were the
cherubim of glory overshadowing the
mercy seat."

HEBREWS 9:3–5a

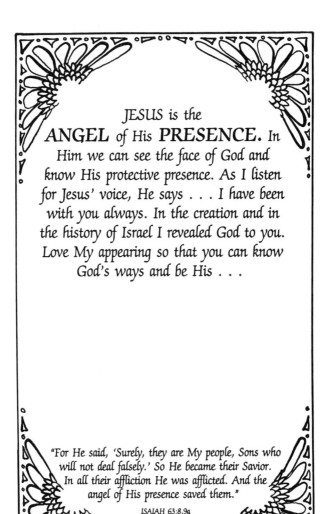

JESUS is the
ANGEL of His **PRESENCE.** In
Him we can see the face of God and
know His protective presence. As I listen
for Jesus' voice, He says . . . I have been
with you always. In the creation and in
the history of Israel I revealed God to you.
Love My appearing so that you can know
God's ways and be His . . .

"For He said, 'Surely, they are My people, Sons who
will not deal falsely.' So He became their Savior.
In all their affliction He was afflicted. And the
angel of His presence saved them."

ISAIAH 63:8,9a

JESUS is the
ADVOCATE.

"He is able to save forever those who draw near to God through Him, since He always lives to make intercession for them" (Hebrews 7:25). Jesus speaks to me today with these thoughts . . . Satan is accusing and condemning you right now before God. I stand there covering you with My love. Please stand with Me and cover both yourself and those who have hurt you with My love and your will to forgive. Every human is fragile and easily crushed by condemnation. I am gentle . . .

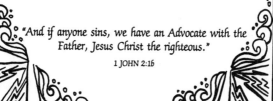

"And if anyone sins, we have an Advocate with the Father, Jesus Christ the righteous."

1 JOHN 2:1b

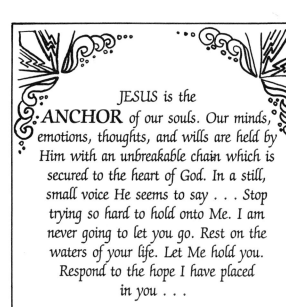

JESUS is the
ANCHOR of our souls. Our minds,
emotions, thoughts, and wills are held by
Him with an unbreakable chain which is
secured to the heart of God. In a still,
small voice He seems to say . . . Stop
trying so hard to hold onto Me. I am
never going to let you go. Rest on the
waters of your life. Let Me hold you.
Respond to the hope I have placed
in you . . .

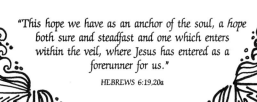

"This hope we have as an anchor of the soul, a hope
both sure and steadfast and one which enters
within the veil, where Jesus has entered as a
forerunner for us."

HEBREWS 6:19,20a

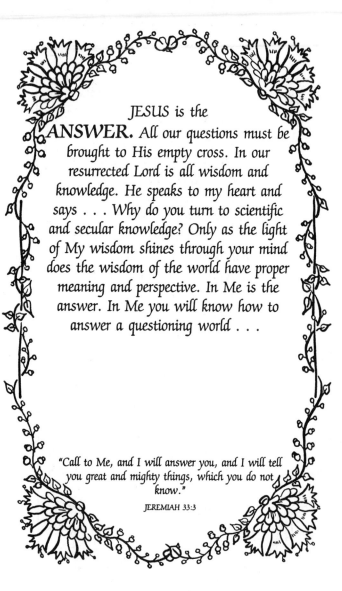

JESUS is the
ANSWER. All our questions must be
brought to His empty cross. In our
resurrected Lord is all wisdom and
knowledge. He speaks to my heart and
says . . . Why do you turn to scientific
and secular knowledge? Only as the light
of My wisdom shines through your mind
does the wisdom of the world have proper
meaning and perspective. In Me is the
answer. In Me you will know how to
answer a questioning world . . .

"Call to Me, and I will answer you, and I will tell
you great and mighty things, which you do not
know."

JEREMIAH 33:3

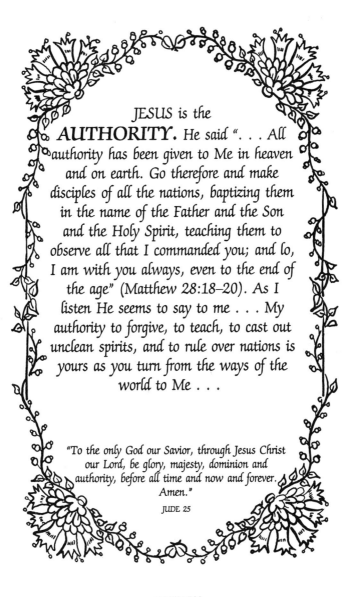

JESUS is the
AUTHORITY. He said ". . . All authority has been given to Me in heaven and on earth. Go therefore and make disciples of all the nations, baptizing them in the name of the Father and the Son and the Holy Spirit, teaching them to observe all that I commanded you; and lo, I am with you always, even to the end of the age" (Matthew 28:18–20). As I listen He seems to say to me . . . My authority to forgive, to teach, to cast out unclean spirits, and to rule over nations is yours as you turn from the ways of the world to Me . . .

"To the only God our Savior, through Jesus Christ our Lord, be glory, majesty, dominion and authority, before all time and now and forever. Amen."

JUDE 25

JESUS is the
APPLE TREE.

In His Presence we find shade, rest, beauty, fragrance, and nourishing, sweet fruit. He says today . . . I love you with an everlasting love. Come to Me. Be filled and refreshed with My goodness. Taste and see that the Lord is good . . .

"Like an apple tree among the trees of the forest, So is my beloved among the young men. In his shade I took great delight and sat down. And his fruit was sweet to my taste."

SONG OF SOLOMON 2:3

JESUS is the
AXE. His Word prunes us and makes us clean of every dead and rotten thing. He speaks in my heart and says . . . I do not delight in hurting you. Like a surgeon I carefully cut away everything in you which could destroy you. Then I gently heal the wounded place so that the fruit you bear will be pleasing to God. Today let your neighbors receive from you love, joy, peace, patience, kindness, faithfulness, goodness, and self-control . . .

"And the axe is already laid at the root of the trees; every tree therefore that does not bear good fruit is cut down and thrown into the fire."

MATTHEW 3:10

JESUS is the
AVENGER. His blood was given to
avenge every wrong done to us, His
brothers and sisters. Now He says to us
. . . When someone hurts you or those
you love, release the wound to Me for
healing. Give the one who hurt you to
Me; pray for him to be forgiven. Say,
"Father forgive him; he didn't know he
was dealing with You." That prayer
releases My power to work in his life to
bring him to Me. In Me your only
motivation is that all men everywhere
come to know My love . . .

"Never take your own revenge, beloved . . . for it is
written, 'vengeance is mine. I will repay, says the
Lord.' but if your enemy is hungry, feed him,
and if he is thirsty give him a drink; for in
so doing you will heap coals on his
head. "

ROMANS 12:19,20

JESUS is the
AMEN. He is the great "YES" to all God's promises to us. He says . . . Come to Me so that you can see yourself as you really are. My gifts to you are great, but are costly to your "self." Yes, you can be glad to die to self for My love has more for you than you can ask or think . . .

"The Amen, the faithful and true Witness, the Beginning of the creation of God, says this: 'I advise you to buy from Me gold . . . white garments and eyesalve. Those whom I love, I reprove and discipline; be zealous . . . repent . . . open the door . . . sit down with Me on My throne.'"

REVELATION 3:146,18–21

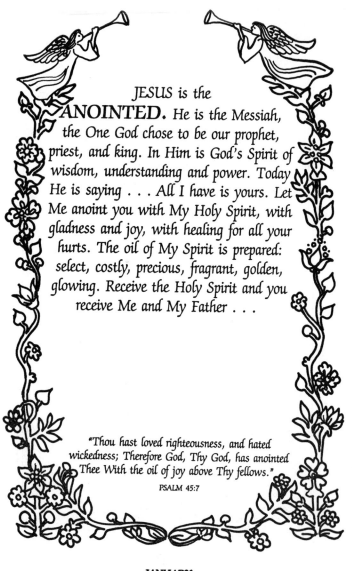

JESUS is the **ANOINTED.** He is the Messiah, the One God chose to be our prophet, priest, and king. In Him is God's Spirit of wisdom, understanding and power. Today He is saying . . . All I have is yours. Let Me anoint you with My Holy Spirit, with gladness and joy, with healing for all your hurts. The oil of My Spirit is prepared: select, costly, precious, fragrant, golden, glowing. Receive the Holy Spirit and you receive Me and My Father . . .

"Thou hast loved righteousness, and hated wickedness; Therefore God, Thy God, has anointed Thee With the oil of joy above Thy fellows."

PSALM 45:7

JESUS is the
ANGEL of the LORD. He is the
messenger of God to us, full of flaming
beauty and awesome power to overcome
our enemies. JESUS says . . . My coming
is soon. Be ready. Let your life be in an
attitude of praise and especially earnest
prayer for those who don't know Me.
Pray that the earth be filled with the
knowledge of God as the waters cover the
sea. Pray that laborers with burning zeal
go out to bring all who will come to
Me . . .

"Behold I am going to send an angel before you to
guard you along the way, and to bring you into
the place which I have prepared. Be on your
guard before him and obey his voice."

EXODUS 23:20,21a

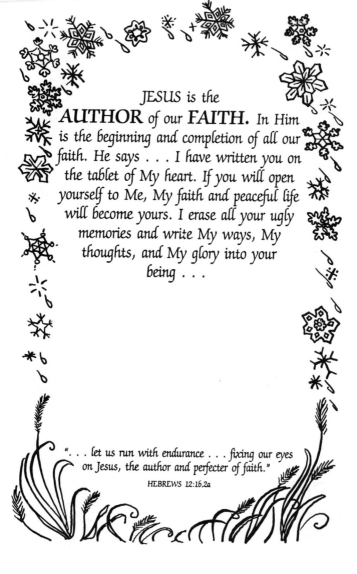

JESUS is the **AUTHOR** of our **FAITH.** In Him is the beginning and completion of all our faith. He says . . . I have written you on the tablet of My heart. If you will open yourself to Me, My faith and peaceful life will become yours. I erase all your ugly memories and write My ways, My thoughts, and My glory into your being . . .

". . . let us run with endurance . . . fixing our eyes on Jesus, the author and perfecter of faith."

HEBREWS 12:1b,2a

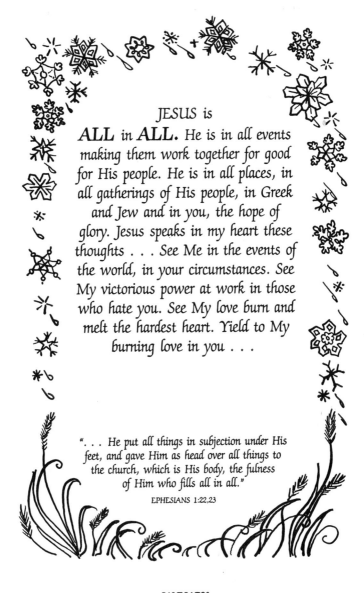

JESUS is

ALL in **ALL.** He is in all events making them work together for good for His people. He is in all places, in all gatherings of His people, in Greek and Jew and in you, the hope of glory. Jesus speaks in my heart these thoughts . . . See Me in the events of the world, in your circumstances. See My victorious power at work in those who hate you. See My love burn and melt the hardest heart. Yield to My burning love in you . . .

". . . He put all things in subjection under His feet, and gave Him as head over all things to the church, which is His body, the fulness of Him who fills all in all."

EPHESIANS 1:22,23

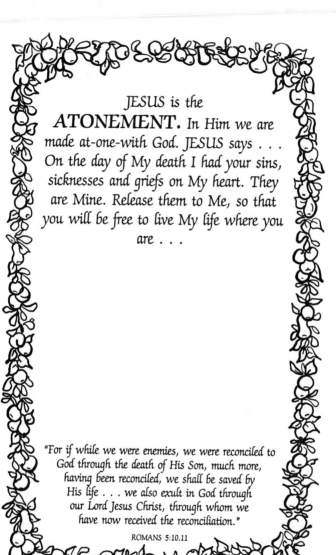

JESUS is the
ATONEMENT. In Him we are
made at-one-with God. JESUS says . . .
On the day of My death I had your sins,
sicknesses and griefs on My heart. They
are Mine. Release them to Me, so that
you will be free to live My life where you
are . . .

"For if while we were enemies, we were reconciled to
God through the death of His Son, much more,
having been reconciled, we shall be saved by
His life . . . we also exult in God through
our Lord Jesus Christ, through whom we
have now received the reconciliation."

ROMANS 5:10,11

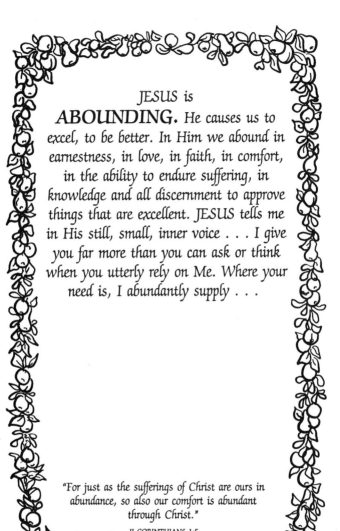

JESUS is

ABOUNDING. He causes us to
excel, to be better. In Him we abound in
earnestness, in love, in faith, in comfort,
in the ability to endure suffering, in
knowledge and all discernment to approve
things that are excellent. JESUS tells me
in His still, small, inner voice . . . I give
you far more than you can ask or think
when you utterly rely on Me. Where your
need is, I abundantly supply . . .

"For just as the sufferings of Christ are ours in
abundance, so also our comfort is abundant
through Christ."

II CORINTHIANS 1:5

JESUS is our
BREAD. Bread is considered a
necessity by all peoples. Jesus indicates
that we all need to take Him into
ourselves in order to live. He speaks to
my heart and says . . . As you eat of the
bread of My Presence daily, you and I
become one flesh, one mind, one spirit.
You will grow in Me and share this food
with hungry ones all around you.
Together we will eat bread in the
Kingdom of heaven . . .

"Jesus said to them, 'I am the bread of life; he who
comes to Me shall not hunger, and he who
believes in Me shall never thirst.' "

JOHN 6:35

JESUS is our
BROTHER. By Him we have been
adopted into God's everlasting family.
Today He says . . . Stay with Me. Spend
time with Me so that I can show you My
Word, My will for you. Then let Me love
your brothers and sisters through you. Let
Me forgive them through you. Let Me
appreciate, honor, and esteem them
through you. Your light will shine and
you will know you are part of My
family . . .

"For whoever does the will of God, he is My brother
and sister and mother."

MARK 3:35

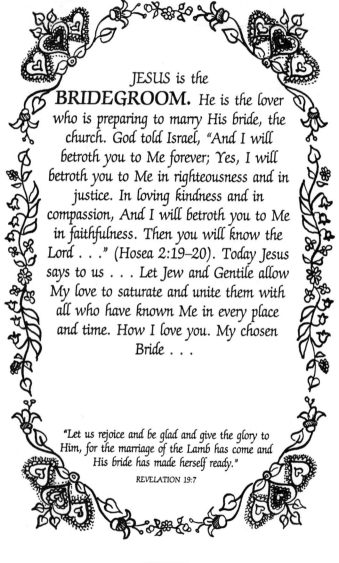

JESUS is the
BRIDEGROOM. He is the lover who is preparing to marry His bride, the church. God told Israel, "And I will betroth you to Me forever; Yes, I will betroth you to Me in righteousness and in justice. In loving kindness and in compassion, And I will betroth you to Me in faithfulness. Then you will know the Lord . . ." (Hosea 2:19–20). Today Jesus says to us . . . Let Jew and Gentile allow My love to saturate and unite them with all who have known Me in every place and time. How I love you. My chosen Bride . . .

"Let us rejoice and be glad and give the glory to Him, for the marriage of the Lamb has come and His bride has made herself ready."

REVELATION 19:7

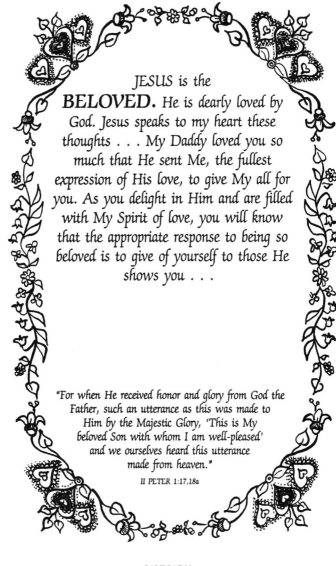

JESUS is the

BELOVED. He is dearly loved by God. Jesus speaks to my heart these thoughts . . . My Daddy loved you so much that He sent Me, the fullest expression of His love, to give My all for you. As you delight in Him and are filled with My Spirit of love, you will know that the appropriate response to being so beloved is to give of yourself to those He shows you . . .

"For when He received honor and glory from God the Father, such an utterance as this was made to Him by the Majestic Glory, 'This is My beloved Son with whom I am well-pleased' and we ourselves heard this utterance made from heaven."

II PETER 1:17,18a

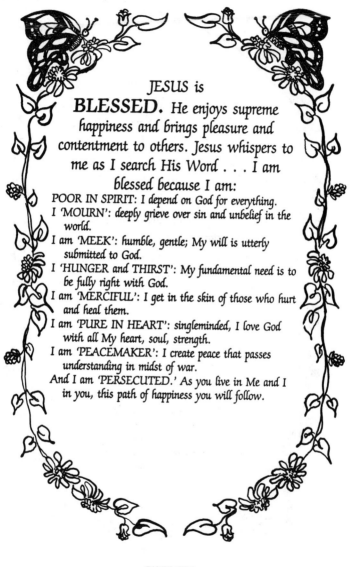

JESUS is

BLESSED. He enjoys supreme
happiness and brings pleasure and
contentment to others. Jesus whispers to
me as I search His Word . . . I am
blessed because I am:

POOR IN SPIRIT: I depend on God for everything.

I 'MOURN': deeply grieve over sin and unbelief in the
world.

I am 'MEEK': humble, gentle; My will is utterly
submitted to God.

I 'HUNGER and THIRST': My fundamental need is to
be fully right with God.

I am 'MERCIFUL': I get in the skin of those who hurt
and heal them.

I am 'PURE IN HEART': singleminded, I love God
with all My heart, soul, strength.

I am 'PEACEMAKER': I create peace that passes
understanding in midst of war.

And I am 'PERSECUTED.' As you live in Me and I
in you, this path of happiness you will follow.

JESUS is the
BLESSER. Because He freely gave
His life for us, we are cleansed and
forgiven. Jesus set us free to be truly all
He designed us to be. With Mary we
say, "From this time on all generations
will count me blessed!" Jesus says in
the quietness of my heart . . . Your
happiness in Me is not like that of the
world. In the world you will have
temptations and persecutions. In the
midst of these your joy will be full and
running over . . .

"Christ redeemed us from the curse of the Law,
having become a curse for us—for it is written,
'CURSED IS EVERYONE WHO HANGS
ON A TREE '—in order that in Christ
Jesus the blessing of Abraham might
come to the Gentiles, so that we
might receive the promise of the
Spirit."

GALATIANS 3:13–14

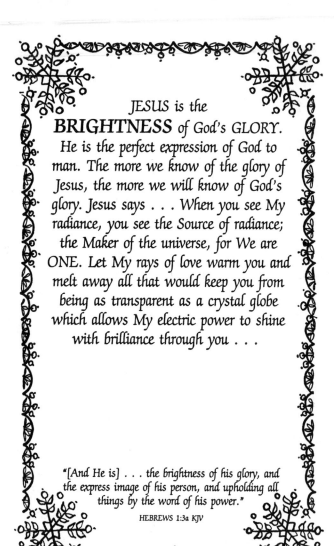

JESUS is the
BRIGHTNESS of God's GLORY.
He is the perfect expression of God to
man. The more we know of the glory of
Jesus, the more we will know of God's
glory. Jesus says . . . When you see My
radiance, you see the Source of radiance;
the Maker of the universe, for We are
ONE. Let My rays of love warm you and
melt away all that would keep you from
being as transparent as a crystal globe
which allows My electric power to shine
with brilliance through you . . .

"[And He is] . . . the brightness of his glory, and
the express image of his person, and upholding all
things by the word of his power."

HEBREWS 1:3a KJV

JESUS is the
BRIGHT and MORNING STAR. Just as the morning light dispels the darkness and fog, so the light of Jesus illuminates our lives. Jesus says . . . Through the clouds of fear and despair which smother those of this world, see that My glory, My shining Presence, which is peace and joy, have come. Let Me penetrate the gloom in your life right now so that you will see through the darkness in others and warm them with My light . . .

"I am the root and the offspring of David, the bright morning star. And the Spirit and the bride say, come. And let the one who hears say, come. And let the one who is thirsty come; let the one who wishes take the water of life without cost."

REVELATION 22:16b–17

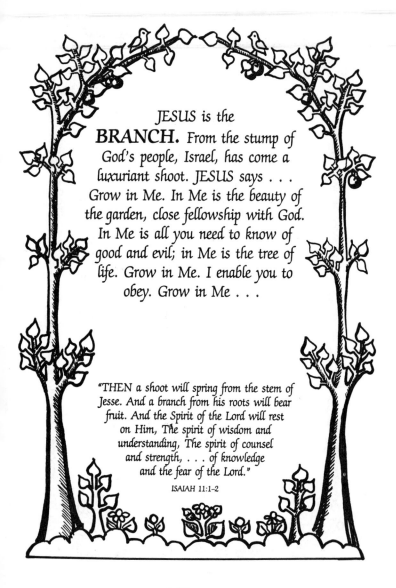

JESUS is the
BRANCH. From the stump of
God's people, Israel, has come a
luxuriant shoot. JESUS says . . .
Grow in Me. In Me is the beauty of
the garden, close fellowship with God.
In Me is all you need to know of
good and evil; in Me is the tree of
life. Grow in Me. I enable you to
obey. Grow in Me . . .

"THEN a shoot will spring from the stem of
Jesse. And a branch from his roots will bear
fruit. And the Spirit of the Lord will rest
on Him, The spirit of wisdom and
understanding, The spirit of counsel
and strength, . . . of knowledge
and the fear of the Lord."

ISAIAH 11:1–2

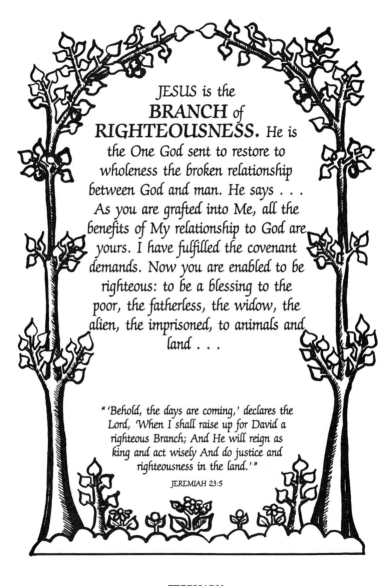

JESUS is the
BRANCH of
RIGHTEOUSNESS. He is
the One God sent to restore to
wholeness the broken relationship
between God and man. He says . . .
As you are grafted into Me, all the
benefits of My relationship to God are
yours. I have fulfilled the covenant
demands. Now you are enabled to be
righteous: to be a blessing to the
poor, the fatherless, the widow, the
alien, the imprisoned, to animals and
land . . .

" 'Behold, the days are coming,' declares the
Lord, 'When I shall raise up for David a
righteous Branch; And He will reign as
king and act wisely And do justice and
righteousness in the land.' "

JEREMIAH 23:5

JESUS is the
BABE. Though He existed in the form
of God He did not grasp onto His high
position, but emptied Himself and became
a tiny baby born in a barn of a young
Jewish woman. JESUS says . . . If you
want to be like Me, you must be born
again. This involves counting all you are
and possess as nothing so that My life
can reign in you. Yield your hopes,
ambitions, abilities to My will. Allow Me
to work My way in you; you will be
glad . . .

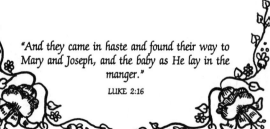

"And they came in haste and found their way to
Mary and Joseph, and the baby as He lay in the
manger."

LUKE 2:16

JESUS is the
BISHOP. He is our overseer and
guardian of our souls. JESUS says . . . I
am with you in every pain and hurt in
your life. I have taken these on Myself so
that you can be free to praise and worship
God. Give Me your sin, sickness, and
griefs so that I can heal you and lead you
in My paths perfect for you . . .

"Who his own self bare our sins in his own body on
the tree, that we, being dead to sins, should live
unto righteousness: by whose stripes ye were
healed. For ye were as sheep going astray;
but are now returned unto the Shepherd
and Bishop of your souls."

I PETER 2:24–25 KJV

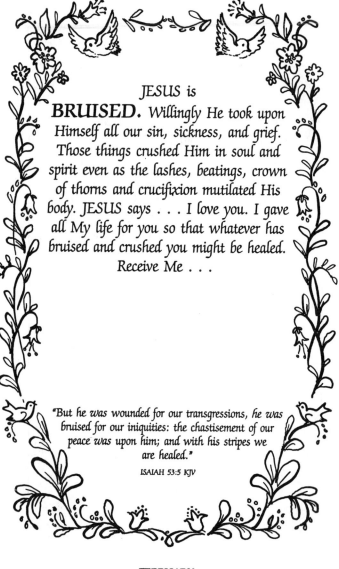

JESUS is

BRUISED. Willingly He took upon
Himself all our sin, sickness, and grief.
Those things crushed Him in soul and
spirit even as the lashes, beatings, crown
of thorns and crucifixion mutilated His
body. JESUS says . . . I love you. I gave
all My life for you so that whatever has
bruised and crushed you might be healed.
Receive Me . . .

"But he was wounded for our transgressions, he was
bruised for our iniquities: the chastisement of our
peace was upon him; and with his stripes we
are healed."

ISAIAH 53:5 KJV

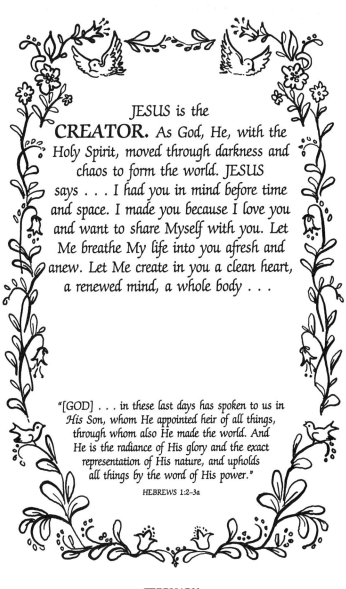

JESUS is the
CREATOR. As God, He, with the
Holy Spirit, moved through darkness and
chaos to form the world. JESUS
says . . . I had you in mind before time
and space. I made you because I love you
and want to share Myself with you. Let
Me breathe My life into you afresh and
anew. Let Me create in you a clean heart,
a renewed mind, a whole body . . .

"[GOD] . . . in these last days has spoken to us in
His Son, whom He appointed heir of all things,
through whom also He made the world. And
He is the radiance of His glory and the exact
representation of His nature, and upholds
all things by the word of His power."

HEBREWS 1:2–3a

JESUS is the
CHRIST. He is God come to us in
flesh as our suffering servant/king. JESUS
says . . . All that I did for those in
Galilee and in Jerusalem I offer to do for
you. Be forgiven, healed, set free, and
empowered with My Holy Spirit. Enter
into Me, the narrow way, and be a part
of My Kingdom coming . . .

" She said to Him, 'Yes, Lord; I have believed that
You are the Christ, the Son of God, even He who
comes into the world.' "

JOHN 11:27

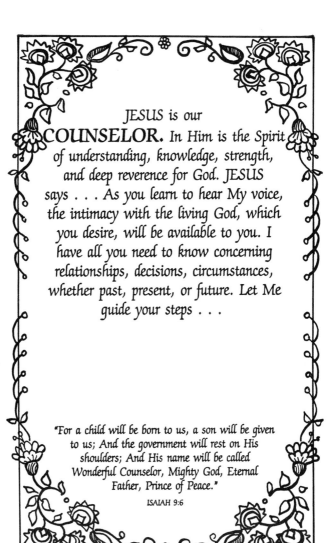

JESUS is our
COUNSELOR. In Him is the Spirit
of understanding, knowledge, strength,
and deep reverence for God. JESUS
says . . . As you learn to hear My voice,
the intimacy with the living God, which
you desire, will be available to you. I
have all you need to know concerning
relationships, decisions, circumstances,
whether past, present, or future. Let Me
guide your steps . . .

"For a child will be born to us, a son will be given
to us; And the government will rest on His
shoulders; And His name will be called
Wonderful Counselor, Mighty God, Eternal
Father, Prince of Peace."

ISAIAH 9:6

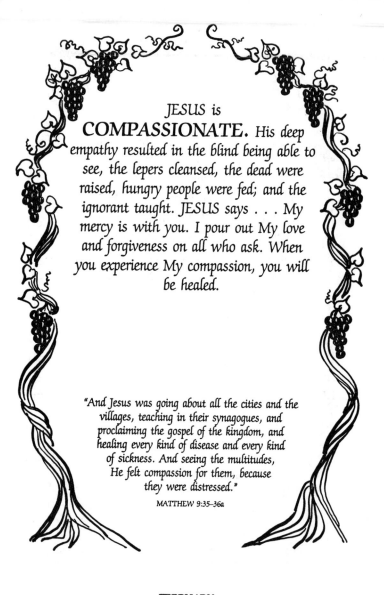

JESUS is
COMPASSIONATE. His deep
empathy resulted in the blind being able to
see, the lepers cleansed, the dead were
raised, hungry people were fed; and the
ignorant taught. JESUS says . . . My
mercy is with you. I pour out My love
and forgiveness on all who ask. When
you experience My compassion, you will
be healed.

"And Jesus was going about all the cities and the
villages, teaching in their synagogues, and
proclaiming the gospel of the kingdom, and
healing every kind of disease and every kind
of sickness. And seeing the multitudes,
He felt compassion for them, because
they were distressed."

MATTHEW 9:35–36a

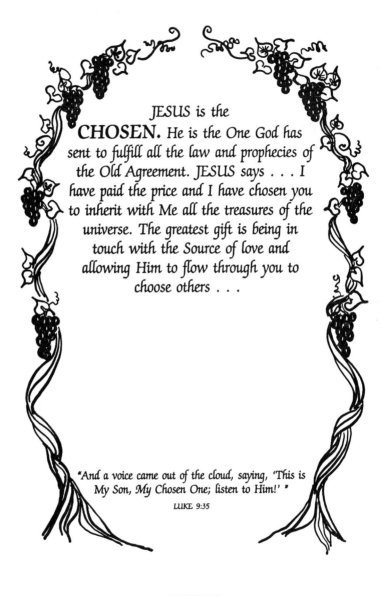

JESUS is the
CHOSEN. He is the One God has
sent to fulfill all the law and prophecies of
the Old Agreement. JESUS says . . . I
have paid the price and I have chosen you
to inherit with Me all the treasures of the
universe. The greatest gift is being in
touch with the Source of love and
allowing Him to flow through you to
choose others . . .

"And a voice came out of the cloud, saying, 'This is
My Son, My Chosen One; listen to Him!' "

LUKE 9:35

JESUS is the
CARPENTER.

He is a skilled craftsman, designer, and builder. JESUS says . . . I am shaping even now the yoke for you that is easy and light. I have sharpened the plow, which is the tool for your work in My harvest. And there is a cross for you on which all of your "self" must die. I offer these to you with nail-pierced hands . . .

"'Is not this the carpenter, the son of Mary, and brother of James, and Joses, and Judas, and Simon? Are not His sisters here with us?' And they took offense at him."

MARK 6:3

JESUS is the
CAPTAIN.

He is the head person, chief, general, governor, keeper, Lord, taskmaster, prince, principal, and ruler. Thousands follow His leadership and obey Him without question. JESUS says . . . I have called you to follow Me. The sword of My Spirit must pierce you first to remove everything in you not of Me. Then you can move in My power, as I direct, to establish My rule in your family, in your place of work, in your community and world . . .

" . . . behold, a man was standing opposite him with his sword drawn in his hand, and Joshua went to him and said to him, 'Are you for us or for our adversaries?' And he said, 'No, rather I . . . come now as captain of the host of the LORD.' "

JOSHUA 5:13b,14

JESUS is the
CANDLESTICK.
He is the seven-branched lampstand
which burns perpetually with the
sevenfold Spirit of God: "The spirit of
wisdom and understanding, The spirit of
counsel and strength, The spirit of
knowledge and the fear of the Lord . . .
and righteousness . . ." (Isaiah 11:2–4a).
"Every good thing bestowed and every
perfect gift is from above, coming down
from the Father of lights, with whom
there is no variation, or shifting shadow"
(James 1:17). JESUS says . . . Ask My
Father for My gifts of light. I want you
to be blessed and shine with My Spirit of
widsom . . .

"And the city has no need of the sun or of the moon
to shine upon it, for the glory of God has
illumined it, and its lamp is the Lamb. And
the nations shall walk by its light."

REVELATION 21:23–24a

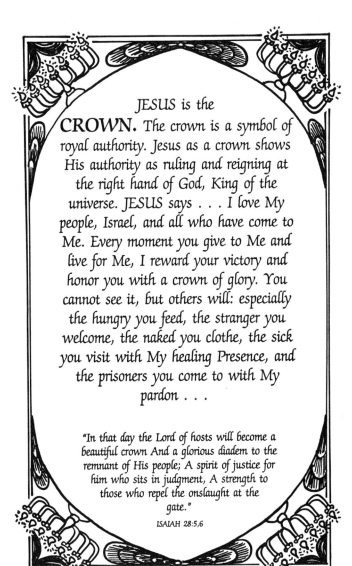

JESUS is the
CROWN. The crown is a symbol of royal authority. Jesus as a crown shows His authority as ruling and reigning at the right hand of God, King of the universe. JESUS says . . . I love My people, Israel, and all who have come to Me. Every moment you give to Me and live for Me, I reward your victory and honor you with a crown of glory. You cannot see it, but others will: especially the hungry you feed, the stranger you welcome, the naked you clothe, the sick you visit with My healing Presence, and the prisoners you come to with My pardon . . .

"In that day the Lord of hosts will become a beautiful crown And a glorious diadem to the remnant of His people; A spirit of justice for him who sits in judgment, A strength to those who repel the onslaught at the gate."

ISAIAH 28:5,6

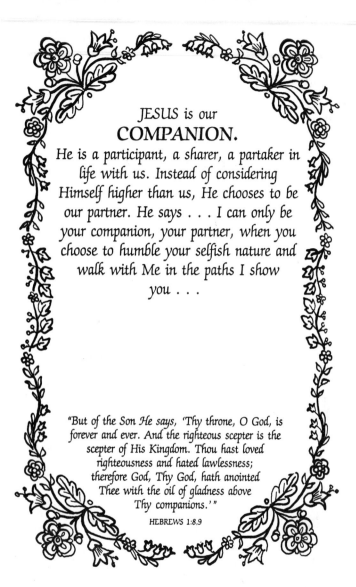

JESUS is our
COMPANION.
He is a participant, a sharer, a partaker in
life with us. Instead of considering
Himself higher than us, He chooses to be
our partner. He says . . . I can only be
your companion, your partner, when you
choose to humble your selfish nature and
walk with Me in the paths I show
you . . .

"But of the Son He says, 'Thy throne, O God, is
forever and ever. And the righteous scepter is the
scepter of His Kingdom. Thou hast loved
righteousness and hated lawlessness;
therefore God, Thy God, hath anointed
Thee with the oil of gladness above
Thy companions.' "

HEBREWS 1:8,9

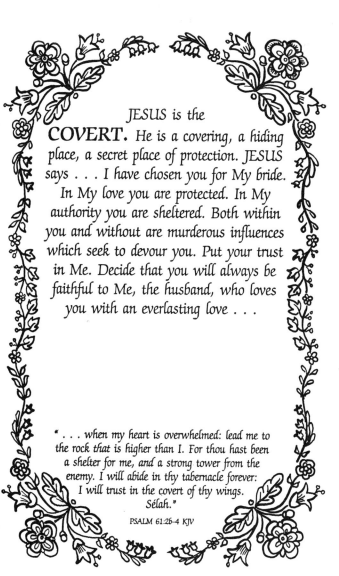

JESUS is the

COVERT. He is a covering, a hiding place, a secret place of protection. JESUS says . . . I have chosen you for My bride. In My love you are protected. In My authority you are sheltered. Both within you and without are murderous influences which seek to devour you. Put your trust in Me. Decide that you will always be faithful to Me, the husband, who loves you with an everlasting love . . .

" . . . when my heart is overwhelmed: lead me to the rock that is higher than I. For thou hast been a shelter for me, and a strong tower from the enemy. I will abide in thy tabernacle forever: I will trust in the covert of thy wings. Sélah."

PSALM 61:2b–4 KJV

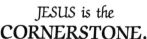

JESUS is the
CORNERSTONE.
He is the basic element in the temple of
the Lord of which we are a part. He is
the solid rock foundation which is our
strength. JESUS says . . . The foundation
which I have given you is the only way.
Build on it, and you shall be glorious in
My eyes. Reject it and I shall close My
eyes to you . . .

"So then you are no longer strangers and aliens, but
you are fellow citizens with the saints, and are of
God's household, having been built upon the
foundation of the apostles and prophets,
Christ Jesus Himself being the corner
stone, in whom the whole building,
being fitted together, is growing into
a holy temple in the Lord; in
whom you also are being built
together into a dwelling of
God in the Spirit."

EPHESIANS 2:19–22

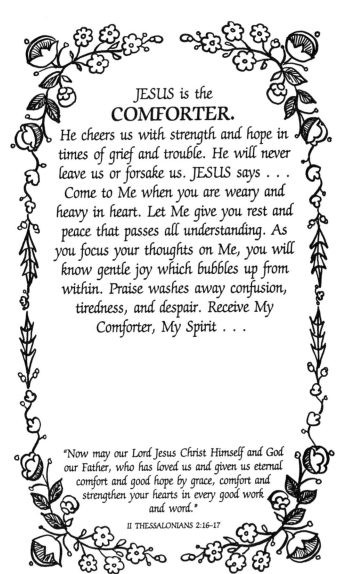

JESUS is the
COMFORTER.

He cheers us with strength and hope in
times of grief and trouble. He will never
leave us or forsake us. JESUS says . . .
Come to Me when you are weary and
heavy in heart. Let Me give you rest and
peace that passes all understanding. As
you focus your thoughts on Me, you will
know gentle joy which bubbles up from
within. Praise washes away confusion,
tiredness, and despair. Receive My
Comforter, My Spirit . . .

"Now may our Lord Jesus Christ Himself and God
our Father, who has loved us and given us eternal
comfort and good hope by grace, comfort and
strengthen your hearts in every good work
and word."

II THESSALONIANS 2:16–17

JESUS is the
CONSOLATION.

He is the consolation of Israel and of all people. He alleviates our sense of grief and loss. JESUS says . . . I came into the world to console you and bring you peace. My strength and comfort shall be your strength and comfort. You have everything on earth you need if you have Me as your Savior . . .

". . . Simeon . . . was righteous and . . . looking for the consolation of Israel . . . it had been revealed to him by the Holy Spirit that he would [see] . . . the Lord's Christ. And he came in the Spirit into the temple; and when the parents brought in the child Jesus, to carry out for Him . . . the Law . . . then he took Him into his arms."

LUKE 2:25–28

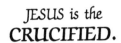

JESUS is the
CRUCIFIED.

Our Father loved us so much that He sent His Son to carry our sins through death. JESUS says . . . I am the blood that pursues you and the body that wants you. Cling to Me and I shall keep you in My bosom . . .

"... let it be known to all of you, and to all the people of Israel, that by the name of Jesus Christ the Nazarene, whom you crucified, whom God raised from the dead—by this name this man stands here before you in good health . . . And there is salvation in no one else; for there is no other name under heaven that has been given among men, by which we must be saved."

ACTS 4:10, 12

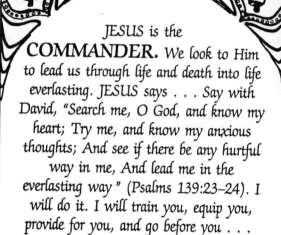

JESUS is the **COMMANDER.** We look to Him to lead us through life and death into life everlasting. JESUS says . . . Say with David, "Search me, O God, and know my heart; Try me, and know my anxious thoughts; And see if there be any hurtful way in me, And lead me in the everlasting way" (Psalms 139:23–24). I will do it. I will train you, equip you, provide for you, and go before you . . .

"Behold, I have made him a witness to the peoples.
A leader and commander for the peoples."

ISAIAH 55:4

JESUS is the
CAPTOR. He gave Himself to the
forces of evil, taking on Himself all our
sins, sickness, and griefs. He entered hell,
overcame Satan, in triumph rose leading
all who would join Him. JESUS says
. . . Victory is yours today in Me. I have
overcome the world. Darkness and demons
flee from you when you stay in My
light . . .

*"Thou hast ascended on high, Thou hast led captive
Thy captives; Thou hast received gifts among
men, Even among the rebellious also, that the
Lord God may dwell there."*

PSALM 68:18

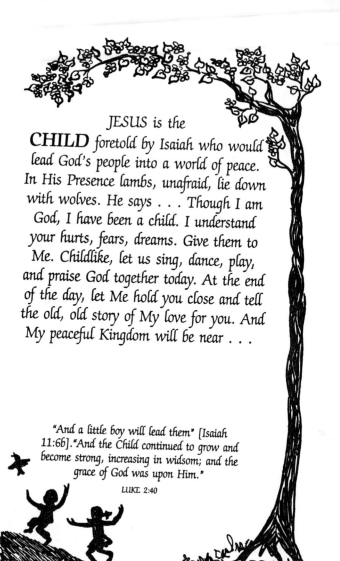

JESUS is the
CHILD foretold by Isaiah who would
lead God's people into a world of peace.
In His Presence lambs, unafraid, lie down
with wolves. He says . . . Though I am
God, I have been a child. I understand
your hurts, fears, dreams. Give them to
Me. Childlike, let us sing, dance, play,
and praise God together today. At the end
of the day, let Me hold you close and tell
the old, old story of My love for you. And
My peaceful Kingdom will be near . . .

"And a little boy will lead them" [Isaiah
11:6b]."And the Child continued to grow and
become strong, increasing in widsom; and the
grace of God was upon Him."

LUKE 2:40

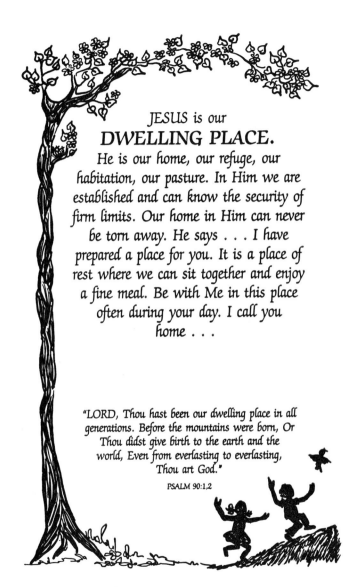

JESUS is our
DWELLING PLACE.
He is our home, our refuge, our
habitation, our pasture. In Him we are
established and can know the security of
firm limits. Our home in Him can never
be torn away. He says . . . I have
prepared a place for you. It is a place of
rest where we can sit together and enjoy
a fine meal. Be with Me in this place
often during your day. I call you
home . . .

"LORD, Thou hast been our dwelling place in all
generations. Before the mountains were born, Or
Thou didst give birth to the earth and the
world, Even from everlasting to everlasting,
Thou art God."

PSALM 90:1,2

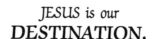

JESUS is our
DESTINATION.

He is the place which is set for us at the
end of life's journey. Our goal is to be
with Him now and forever. He says . . .
Come ". . . to Mount Zion and to the
city of the living God, the heavenly
Jerusalem, and to myriads of angels, to
the general assembly and church of the
first-born who are enrolled in heaven, and
to God, the judge of all, and to the spirits
of righteous men made perfect, and to
Jesus, the mediator of a new
covenant. . ." (Hebrews 12:22–24a).

"In my Father's house are many dwelling places; if it
were not so, I would have told you; for I go to
prepare a place for you . . . I will come again,
and receive you to Myself; that where I am,
there you may be also."

JOHN 14:2,3

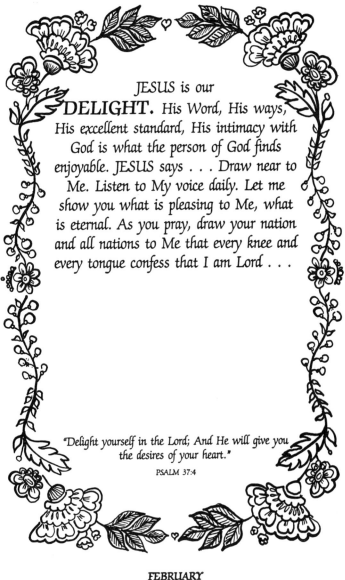

JESUS is our **DELIGHT.** His Word, His ways, His excellent standard, His intimacy with God is what the person of God finds enjoyable. JESUS says . . . Draw near to Me. Listen to My voice daily. Let me show you what is pleasing to Me, what is eternal. As you pray, draw your nation and all nations to Me that every knee and every tongue confess that I am Lord . . .

"Delight yourself in the Lord; And He will give you the desires of your heart."

PSALM 37:4

JESUS is the
DELIVERER. From Egyptian
slavery through the Red Sea, from
Babylonian exile, from Nazi extermination
God has delivered His people, the Jews.
JESUS says . . . I am a Jew. I have
known rejection, suffering, and death even
as My people have. With tenderest love I
stretch out My arms to them. I bid them
receive Me as their own deliverer to
become complete in Me. Y'shua
Ha'Mashiach . . .

"And thus all Israel will be saved; just as it is
written, 'THE DELIVERER WILL COME
FROM ZION, HE WILL REMOVE
UNGODLINESS FROM JACOB . . .' from
the standpoint of God's choice they are
beloved for the sake of the fathers; for
the gifts and the calling of God are
irrevocable."

ROMANS 11:26,28b–29

JESUS is the
DEFENDER. Let all Israel look to
Y'shua Ha'Mashiach for their defense. As
Zechariah, the prophet, said about
him . . .

"In that day the Lord will defend the inhabitants of
Jerusalem, and the one who is feeble among them in
that day will be like David and the house of David will
be like God, like the angel of the LORD before them
. . . And I will pour out on the house of David and on
the inhabitants of Jerusalem, the Spirit of grace and of
supplication, so that they will look on Me whom they
have pierced; and they will mourn for Him, as one
mourns for an only son, and they will weep bitterly for
Him, like the bitter weeping over a first-born."

ZECHARIAH 12:8,10

JESUS is our
DESIRE. The desire of nations is for
wealth, power, and land; yet all these are
in Jesus' hand. We are created so that
Jesus is the fulfillment of our deepest
longings. All we need is in Him. He
says . . . One day I had no beauty that
any would desire Me. All turned away
from the horror of My cross. Through the
ugliness now you see the brilliance of My
love for you—and desire Me . . .

" . . . Thy name, even Thy memory, is the desire of
our souls. At night my soul longs for Thee,
Indeed, my spirit within me seeks Thee
diligently."

ISAIAH 26:8b,9a

FEBRUARY
29

JESUS is the
DEW. As He silently comes to us, we
are refreshed and renewed. Through Him
we are made abundantly fruitful. JESUS
says . . . In Me there is unity with all
others who know Me. I am in your
midst. Look for evidences of My Presence
in others who bear My Name. Thank Me
for the ways I have worked in your life.
Be glad, for My dew is upon you . . .

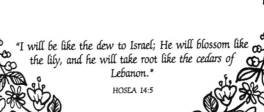

"I will be like the dew to Israel; He will blossom like
the lily, and he will take root like the cedars of
Lebanon."

HOSEA 14:5

JESUS is the
DIVIDER of Nations. Where is the
nation that feeds the hungry, gives water
to the thirsty, welcomes strangers, clothes
the naked, visits the sick and imprisoned?
Where is the country that truly cares
about people? This is the government
which will be part of God's government.
Jesus says . . . Only with God is this
possible. Intercede for your nation to turn
from wicked ways to My ways, so that I
can forgive and heal your land . . .

"And all the nations will be gathered before Him;
and He will separate them from one another, as
the shepherd separates the sheep from the goats;
and He will put the sheep on His right, and
the goats on the left."

MATTHEW 25:32,33

JESUS is the
DAYSMAN. He is the umpire or
mediator between us and God, who
desires that all men may be in right
relation with Himself. Jesus says . . .
Pray for the kings and presidents, military
leaders, judges and police of every nation.
Humble yourself and be an instrument of
peace where you are. My peace I give to
you . . .

"For *he* is not a man, as *I am, that* I should answer
him, *and* we should come together in judgment.
Neither is there any daysman betwixt us."

JOB 9:32,33a, KJV

"For I know *that* my redeemer liveth, and *that* he
shall stand at the latter *day* upon the earth."

JOB 19:25 KJV

"For *there* is one God, and one mediator between God
and men, the man Christ Jesus; Who gave himself
a ransom for all."

I TIMOTHY 2:5,6a KJV

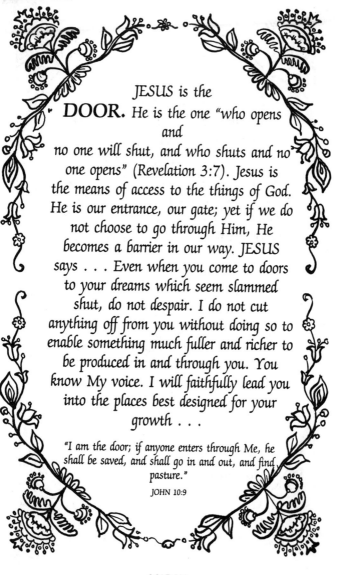

JESUS is the
DOOR. He is the one "who opens and
no one will shut, and who shuts and no
one opens" (Revelation 3:7). Jesus is
the means of access to the things of God.
He is our entrance, our gate; yet if we do
not choose to go through Him, He
becomes a barrier in our way. JESUS
says . . . Even when you come to doors
to your dreams which seem slammed
shut, do not despair. I do not cut
anything off from you without doing so to
enable something much fuller and richer to
be produced in and through you. You
know My voice. I will faithfully lead you
into the places best designed for your
growth . . .

"I am the door; if anyone enters through Me, he
shall be saved, and shall go in and out, and find
pasture."

JOHN 10:9

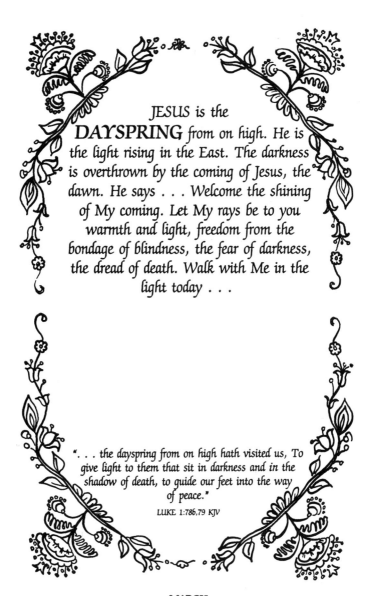

JESUS is the
DAYSPRING from on high. He is
the light rising in the East. The darkness
is overthrown by the coming of Jesus, the
dawn. He says . . . Welcome the shining
of My coming. Let My rays be to you
warmth and light, freedom from the
bondage of blindness, the fear of darkness,
the dread of death. Walk with Me in the
light today . . .

" . . . the dayspring from on high hath visited us, To
give light to them that sit in darkness and in the
shadow of death, to guide our feet into the way
of peace."

LUKE 1:78b,79 KJV

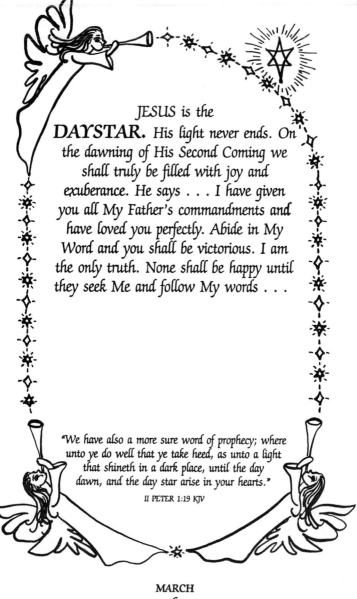

JESUS is the
DAYSTAR. His light never ends. On
the dawning of His Second Coming we
shall truly be filled with joy and
exuberance. He says . . . I have given
you all My Father's commandments and
have loved you perfectly. Abide in My
Word and you shall be victorious. I am
the only truth. None shall be happy until
they seek Me and follow My words . . .

"We have also a more sure word of prophecy; where
unto ye do well that ye take heed, as unto a light
that shineth in a dark place, until the day
dawn, and the day star arise in your hearts."

II PETER 1:19 KJV

MARCH
6

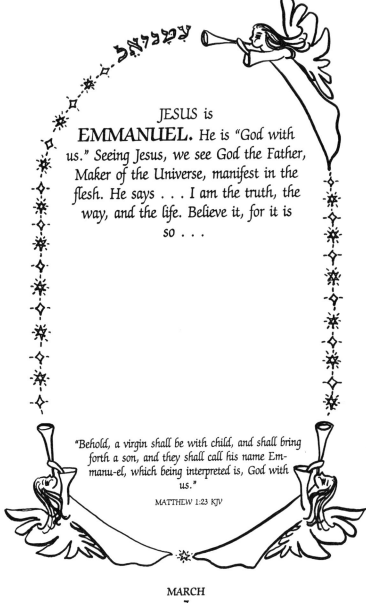

עִמָּנוּאֵל

JESUS is
EMMANUEL. He is "God with us." Seeing Jesus, we see God the Father, Maker of the Universe, manifest in the flesh. He says . . . I am the truth, the way, and the life. Believe it, for it is so . . .

"Behold, a virgin shall be with child, and shall bring forth a son, and they shall call his name Emmanu-el, which being interpreted is, God with us."

MATTHEW 1:23 KJV

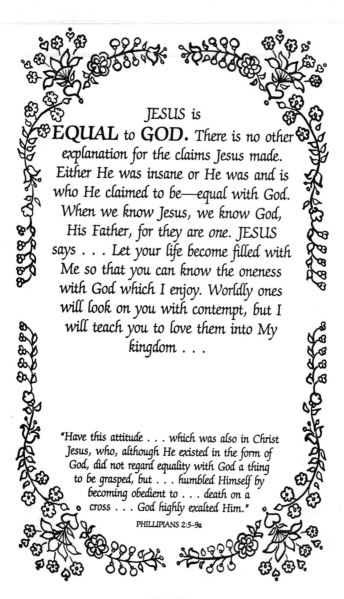

JESUS is
EQUAL to **GOD.** There is no other explanation for the claims Jesus made. Either He was insane or He was and is who He claimed to be—equal with God. When we know Jesus, we know God, His Father, for they are one. JESUS says . . . Let your life become filled with Me so that you can know the oneness with God which I enjoy. Worldly ones will look on you with contempt, but I will teach you to love them into My kingdom . . .

"Have this attitude . . . which was also in Christ Jesus, who, although He existed in the form of God, did not regard equality with God a thing to be grasped, but . . . humbled Himself by becoming obedient to . . . death on a cross . . . God highly exalted Him."

PHILLIPIANS 2:5–9a

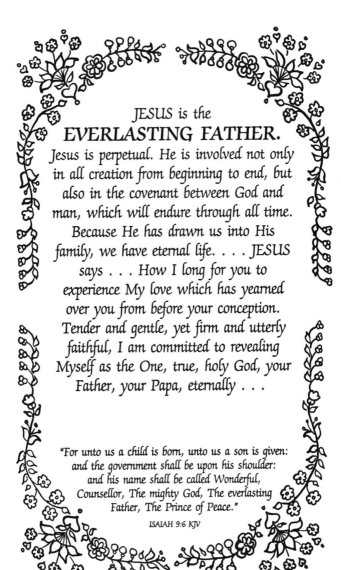

JESUS is the
EVERLASTING FATHER.

Jesus is perpetual. He is involved not only in all creation from beginning to end, but also in the covenant between God and man, which will endure through all time. Because He has drawn us into His family, we have eternal life. . . . JESUS says . . . How I long for you to experience My love which has yearned over you from before your conception. Tender and gentle, yet firm and utterly faithful, I am committed to revealing Myself as the One, true, holy God, your Father, your Papa, eternally . . .

"For unto us a child is born, unto us a son is given: and the government shall be upon his shoulder: and his name shall be called Wonderful, Counsellor, The mighty God, The everlasting Father, The Prince of Peace."

ISAIAH 9:6 KJV

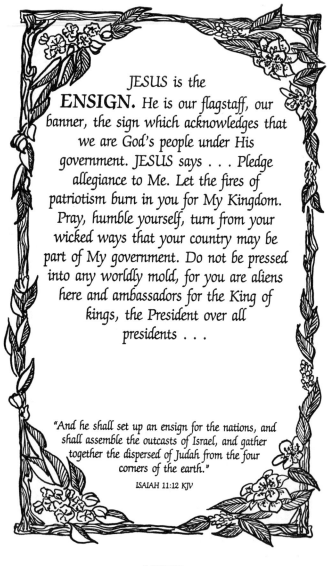

JESUS is the
ENSIGN. He is our flagstaff, our banner, the sign which acknowledges that we are God's people under His government. JESUS says . . . Pledge allegiance to Me. Let the fires of patriotism burn in you for My Kingdom. Pray, humble yourself, turn from your wicked ways that your country may be part of My government. Do not be pressed into any worldly mold, for you are aliens here and ambassadors for the King of kings, the President over all presidents . . .

"And he shall set up an ensign for the nations, and shall assemble the outcasts of Israel, and gather together the dispersed of Judah from the four corners of the earth."

ISAIAH 11:12 KJV

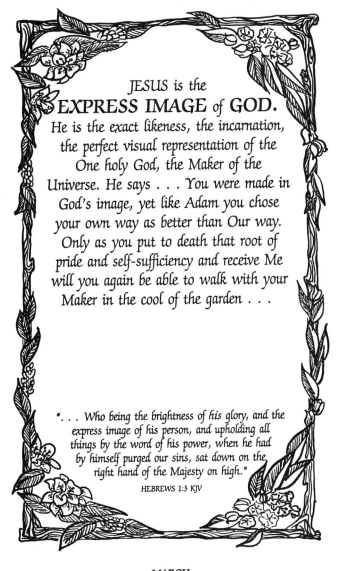

JESUS is the
EXPRESS IMAGE of GOD.

He is the exact likeness, the incarnation,
the perfect visual representation of the
One holy God, the Maker of the
Universe. He says . . . You were made in
God's image, yet like Adam you chose
your own way as better than Our way.
Only as you put to death that root of
pride and self-sufficiency and receive Me
will you again be able to walk with your
Maker in the cool of the garden . . .

" . . . Who being the brightness of *his* glory, and the
express image of his person, and upholding all
things by the word of his power, when he had
by himself purged our sins, sat down on the
right hand of the Majesty on high."

HEBREWS 1:3 KJV

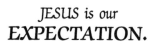

JESUS is our
EXPECTATION.

We can put all our trust and hope in
Him. He says . . . Watch and pray, I tell
My disciples today. Allow My Spirit to
grow you to maturity as the whole
universe groans for the birth of My people.
As a woman waits for her first child,
prepare for My Second Coming—with
joy . . .

"For I know that this shall turn out for my
deliverance through your prayers and the provision
of the Spirit of Jesus Christ, according to my
earnest expectation and hope, that I shall not
be put to shame in anything, but that
with all boldness, Christ shall even
now, as always, be exalted in my
body, whether by life or by
death."

PHILLIPIANS 1:19–20

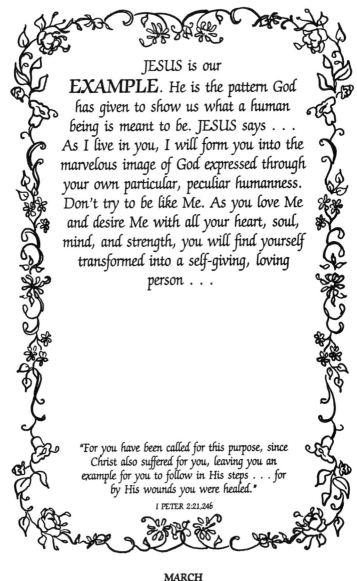

JESUS is our
EXAMPLE. He is the pattern God
has given to show us what a human
being is meant to be. JESUS says . . .
As I live in you, I will form you into the
marvelous image of God expressed through
your own particular, peculiar humanness.
Don't try to be like Me. As you love Me
and desire Me with all your heart, soul,
mind, and strength, you will find yourself
transformed into a self-giving, loving
person . . .

"For you have been called for this purpose, since
Christ also suffered for you, leaving you an
example for you to follow in His steps . . . for
by His wounds you were healed."

I PETER 2:21,24b

JESUS is
ETERNAL. In Him we have
uninterrupted, everlasting intimacy with
God. JESUS says . . . Eat and drink My
nature as your very source of life and
nourishment. In Me death to yourself is
daily, so physical death is but the door
which leads to a deeper, permanent life in
Me. It is glorious . . .

" . . . even as Thou gavest Him authority over all
mankind, that to all whom Thou hast given Him,
He may give eternal life. And this is eternal
life, that they may know Thee, the only true
God, and Jesus Christ whom Thou hast
sent."

JOHN 17:2,3

JESUS is
EXALTED. He is far above all gods
of this earth. Worthy is He of our honor,
worship, and highest praise. He says . . .
I humbled Myself from the glory of heaven
to become a babe born in a manure pile. I
grew up, ministered as God directed, and
died violently on a garbage heap. Because
I humbled Myself, God lifted Me up. He
will do the same for you . . .

". . . God highly exalted Him, and bestowed on
Him the name which is above every name, that at
the name of Jesus every knee should bow, of
those who are in heaven, and on earth, and
under the earth, and that every tongue
should confess that Jesus Christ is
Lord, to the glory of God the
Father."

PHILLIPIANS 2:9–11

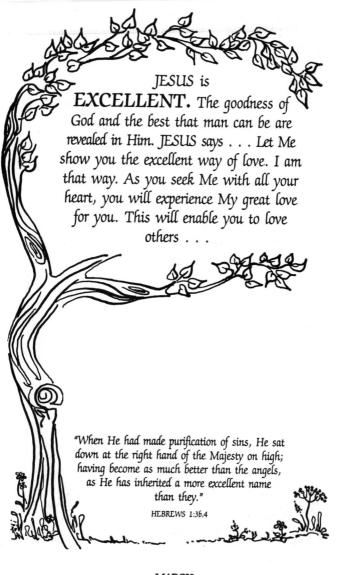

JESUS is
EXCELLENT. The goodness of
God and the best that man can be are
revealed in Him. JESUS says . . . Let Me
show you the excellent way of love. I am
that way. As you seek Me with all your
heart, you will experience My great love
for you. This will enable you to love
others . . .

"When He had made purification of sins, He sat
down at the right hand of the Majesty on high;
having become as much better than the angels,
as He has inherited a more excellent name
than they."

HEBREWS 1:3b,4

JESUS is
EVERLASTING LIFE. The love relationship we have with Jesus flows beyond time and space, uninterrupted, when we believe and obey Him. JESUS says . . . Only in Me can you really know what life is and how sacred. As you live in Me you will appreciate your family, friends, neighbors, and enemies with a holy gratitude . . .

"But whosoever drinketh of the water that I shall give him shall never thirst; but the water that I shall give him shall be in him a well of water springing up into everlasting life."

JOHN 4:14 KJV

JESUS is

ENDURING. Because He remained firm under suffering of the cross, He sits at God's right hand. He encourages us to continue through hardships without giving in. He says . . . The door to eternal joy opens to those who receive from Me the ability to love, even those who hate you. I will lead you through the valley of the shadow of death to yourself, into victorious love . . .

". . . see that ye love one another with a pure heart fervently: Being born again, . . . by the word of God which liveth and abideth forever . . . the word of the Lord endureth forever."

I PETER 1:22b–23,25a KJV

JESUS is the
END. In Him is the right way to live, the goal and completion of all God expects. He says, ". . . hold fast until I come. And he who overcomes, and he who keeps My deeds until the end, TO HIM I WILL GIVE AUTHORITY OVER THE NATIONS . . ." (Revelation 2:25b–26). ". . . I am the Alpha and the Omega, the beginning and the end. I will give to the one who thirsts from the spring of the water of life without cost." (Revelation 21:6b)

"For Christ is the end of the law for righteousness to everyone who believes."
ROMANS 10:4

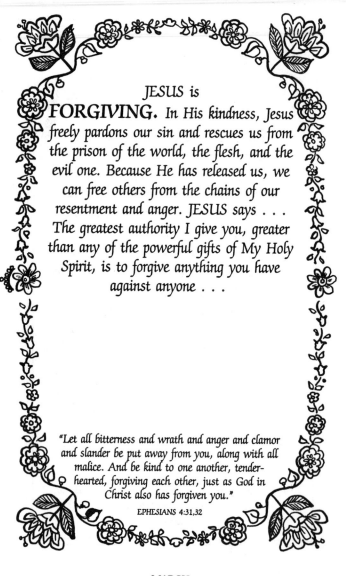

JESUS is
FORGIVING. In His kindness, Jesus
freely pardons our sin and rescues us from
the prison of the world, the flesh, and the
evil one. Because He has released us, we
can free others from the chains of our
resentment and anger. JESUS says . . .
The greatest authority I give you, greater
than any of the powerful gifts of My Holy
Spirit, is to forgive anything you have
against anyone . . .

"Let all bitterness and wrath and anger and clamor
and slander be put away from you, along with all
malice. And be kind to one another, tender-
hearted, forgiving each other, just as God in
Christ also has forgiven you."

EPHESIANS 4:31,32

JESUS is our **FRIEND.** He loved us enough to give His life for us. Now He desires an intimate relationship with us. JESUS says . . . I am your Friend, but are you Mine? Have you laid down your life, hopes, dreams, desires, at the foot of My cross? Have you said, "Lord, what do You want today?" My friend, I want the best for you. That will include plunging into and exploring love for those around you . . .

"This is My commandment, that you love one another, just as I have loved you. Greater love has no one than this, that one lay down his life for his friends. You are My friends, if you do what I command you."

JOHN 15:12–14

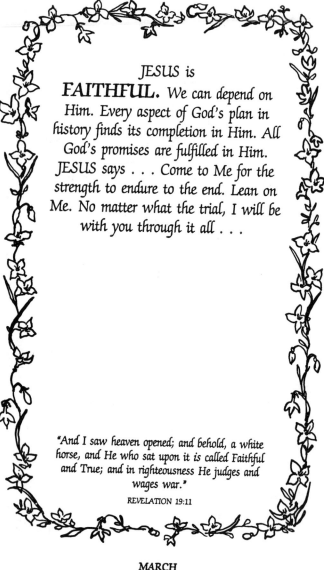

JESUS is

FAITHFUL. We can depend on Him. Every aspect of God's plan in history finds its completion in Him. All God's promises are fulfilled in Him. JESUS says . . . Come to Me for the strength to endure to the end. Lean on Me. No matter what the trial, I will be with you through it all . . .

"And I saw heaven opened; and behold, a white horse, and He who sat upon it is called Faithful and True; and in righteousness He judges and wages war."

REVELATION 19:11

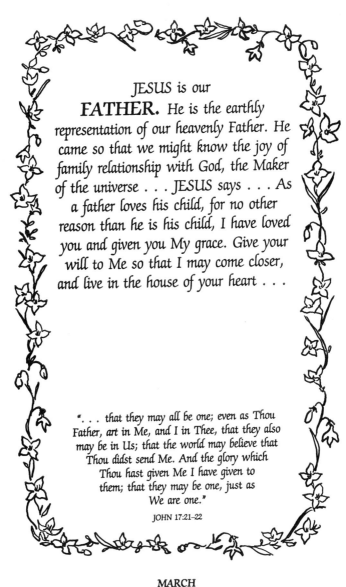

JESUS is our
FATHER. He is the earthly
representation of our heavenly Father. He
came so that we might know the joy of
family relationship with God, the Maker
of the universe . . . JESUS says . . . As
a father loves his child, for no other
reason than he is his child, I have loved
you and given you My grace. Give your
will to Me so that I may come closer,
and live in the house of your heart . . .

". . . that they may all be one; even as Thou
Father, art in Me, and I in Thee, that they also
may be in Us; that the world may believe that
Thou didst send Me. And the glory which
Thou hast given Me I have given to
them; that they may be one, just as
We are one."

JOHN 17:21-22

JESUS is the
FOUNTAIN.
His blood cleanses us and enables us to drink of the life of God. He says . . . Are you thirsty for more of God? Let Me satisfy you. As you fill yourself with Me, I will flow out of your innermost being to bless others with never-ending rivers of living water . . .

"And the children of men take refuge in the shadow of Thy wings. They drink their fill of the abundance of Thy house; And Thou dost give them to drink of the river of Thy delights, For with Thee is the fountain of life; In Thy light we see light."

PSALMS 36:7b–9

JESUS is the

FAIREST. To the eye and the mind of the true believer, Jesus has surpassing beauty. His is a pure, fresh quality which is desirable in every way. He says . . .

As you turn away from worldly loves, you will see the deep love I have for you. I delight in you and want you to be part of that fairest one, My chosen bride . . .

"Behold, thou art fair, my beloved, yea, pleasant: also our bed is green."

SONG OF SOLOMON 1:16 KJV

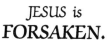

JESUS is
FORSAKEN.

After having complete union with God, our sin, sickness, and grief ripped that relationship apart, leaving Jesus utterly alone on the tree of death. He says . . . I still experience the agony of that hour when you do not turn over to Me everything that separates you from close, warm fellowship with Our Father. I will never leave you nor forsake you; I will enable you to release every burden to Me . . .

"And at the ninth hour Jesus cried out with a loud voice, 'ELOI, ELOI, LAMA SABACHTHANI?' which is translated, 'MY GOD, MY GOD, WHY HAST THOU FORSAKEN ME?' "

MARK 15:34

JESUS is

FIRE. His words burn within us to remove everything in the temple of our lives which is unable to stand the fire of God's eternal presence. He says . . . Present yourself as a living sacrifice so that I can freely burn in you My baptism of fire. Much that fills your life will go quickly. What is left will be pure gold, precious as it is costly . . .

" 'Is not My word like fire?' declares the Lord, 'and like a hammer which shatters a rock?' "

JEREMIAH 23:29

JESUS is the
FRIEND of SINNERS.
How glad we can be that He comes to us
in love when we recognize that we are
estranged from God by our nature and by
our actions, thoughts, and the motives of
our hearts. He says . . . Early I am
seeking you. Do not deny My friendship
by hiding things in yourself that are
wrong. My Word cleanses you so we can
share our hearts openly together
always . . .

"The Son of Man has come eating and drinking; and
you say, 'Behold, a gluttonous man, and a
drunkard, a friend of tax-gatherers and
sinners!' "

LUKE 7:34

JESUS is the
FORERUNNER.
He has gone before us through death into God's unveiled Presence. He announces our coming and prepares our way. He says . . . keep close to Me as you travel through life. I know the dangerous pitfalls and the position of your enemies. Together we will go safely through into eternal glory . . .

"This hope we have as an anchor of the soul, a hope both sure and steadfast and one which enters within the veil, where Jesus has entered as a forerunner for us, having become a high priest forever according to the order of Melchizedek."

HEBREWS 6:19,20

JESUS is the
FINISHER. He has perfected and
completed the faith which He gave us.
JESUS says . . . Look to Me as you go
through the obstacles of life. What I
began in you, I will finish . . .

*" . . . let us lay aside every weight, and the sin
which doth so easily beset us, and let us run with
patience the race that is set before us, Looking
unto Jesus the author and finisher of our
faith . . ."*

HEBREWS 12:1b,2a KJV

JESUS is the
FIRST. He is with God from the beginning of everything that is. Jesus is also through everything and in Him will everything end. He says . . . In Me there is no fear of the unknown. Wherever you go, I have been there first. Hold My hand . . .

"And He laid His right hand upon me, saying, 'Do not be afraid; I am the first and the last, and the living One; and I was dead, and behold, I am alive forevermore, and I have the keys of death and of Hades.' "
REVELATION 1:17b,18

JESUS is the
FIRSTBORN. He is the firstborn of
all creation and Mary's first son. Jesus
went through death before us and is the
first to be raised from the dead. Through
Him we are born into God's family. He
says . . . There is nothing in life or death
that you need to fear. I take care of My
little brothers and sisters . . .

". . . Jesus Christ, the faithful witness, the firstborn
of the dead, and the ruler of the kings of the earth
. . . who loves us, and released us from our
sins by His blood, and He has made us to
be a kingdom, priests to His God and
Father."

REVELATION 1:5–6a

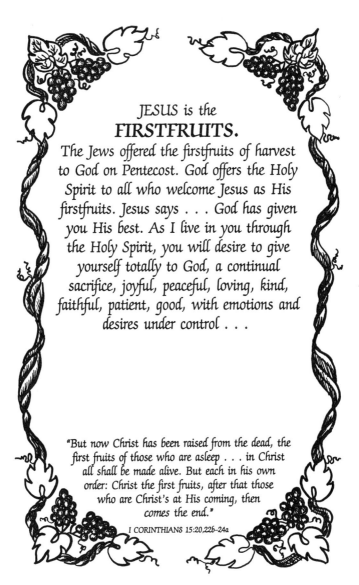

JESUS is the
FIRSTFRUITS.

The Jews offered the firstfruits of harvest to God on Pentecost. God offers the Holy Spirit to all who welcome Jesus as His firstfruits. Jesus says . . . God has given you His best. As I live in you through the Holy Spirit, you will desire to give yourself totally to God, a continual sacrifice, joyful, peaceful, loving, kind, faithful, patient, good, with emotions and desires under control . . .

"But now Christ has been raised from the dead, the first fruits of those who are asleep . . . in Christ all shall be made alive. But each in his own order: Christ the first fruits, after that those who are Christ's at His coming, then comes the end."

I CORINTHIANS 15:20,22b–24a

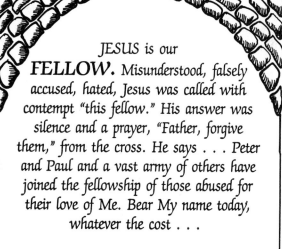

JESUS is our **FELLOW.** Misunderstood, falsely accused, hated, Jesus was called with contempt "this fellow." His answer was silence and a prayer, "Father, forgive them," from the cross. He says . . . Peter and Paul and a vast army of others have joined the fellowship of those abused for their love of Me. Bear My name today, whatever the cost . . .

"At the last came two false witnesses, And said, This *fellow* said, I am able to destroy the temple of God, and to build it in three days . . . But Jesus held his peace."

MATTHEW 26:60b–61,63a KJV

JESUS is our
FOUNDATION.

On the precious stone of Jesus we build
our lives as a holy temple. The fire of His
Spirit burns away every part of us which
is not worthy of being God's house. He
says . . . Rejoice in the burning. Be glad
that the Master Builder has chosen you
and is fitting you securely to Me . . .

"For no man can lay a foundation other than the one
which is laid, which is Jesus Christ."

I CORINTHIANS 3:11

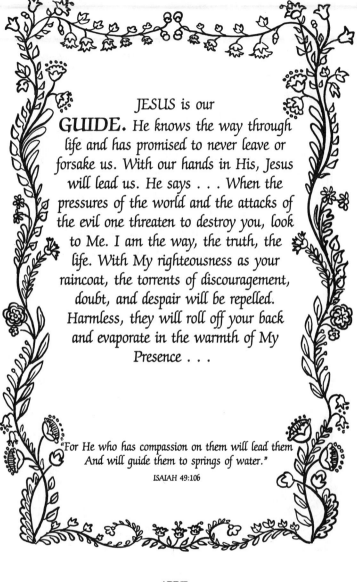

JESUS is our
GUIDE. He knows the way through life and has promised to never leave or forsake us. With our hands in His, Jesus will lead us. He says . . . When the pressures of the world and the attacks of the evil one threaten to destroy you, look to Me. I am the way, the truth, the life. With My righteousness as your raincoat, the torrents of discouragement, doubt, and despair will be repelled. Harmless, they will roll off your back and evaporate in the warmth of My Presence . . .

"For He who has compassion on them will lead them
And will guide them to springs of water."

ISAIAH 49:10b

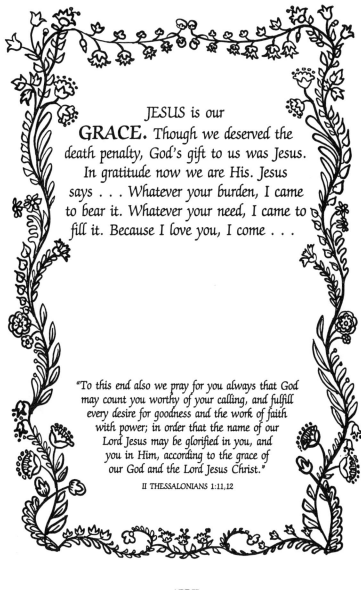

JESUS is our
GRACE. Though we deserved the
death penalty, God's gift to us was Jesus.
In gratitude now we are His. Jesus
says . . . Whatever your burden, I came
to bear it. Whatever your need, I came to
fill it. Because I love you, I come . . .

"To this end also we pray for you always that God
may count you worthy of your calling, and fulfill
every desire for goodness and the work of faith
with power; in order that the name of our
Lord Jesus may be glorified in you, and
you in Him, according to the grace of
our God and the Lord Jesus Christ."

II THESSALONIANS 1:11,12

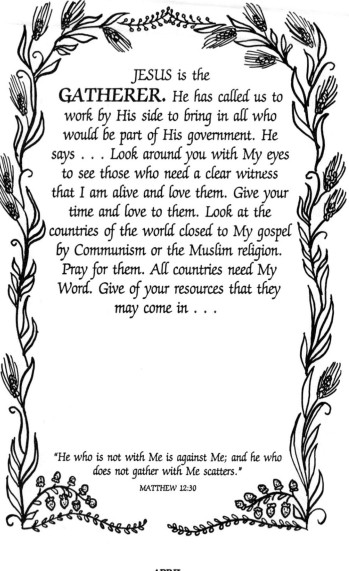

JESUS is the
GATHERER. He has called us to
work by His side to bring in all who
would be part of His government. He
says . . . Look around you with My eyes
to see those who need a clear witness
that I am alive and love them. Give your
time and love to them. Look at the
countries of the world closed to My gospel
by Communism or the Muslim religion.
Pray for them. All countries need My
Word. Give of your resources that they
may come in . . .

"He who is not with Me is against Me; and he who
does not gather with Me scatters."

MATTHEW 12:30

JESUS is

GREAT. In majesty, in power, in compassion we see the greatness of God in Jesus. He says . . . All the riches and honor of heaven did not make Me worthy of your praise. I was willing to come to you as a helpless baby. I suffered the difficulties of growing up, of finding God's will, of being obedient. I died for you, and live again; so now I am great. Will you decrease so that I can increase in you?

"... and you shall name Him Jesus. He will be great, and will be called the Son of the Most High; and the Lord God will give Him the throne of His father David."

LUKE 1:31b–32

JESUS is our
GIFT. God freely gave Himself in Jesus
to all who would receive. He says . . .
Open Me, the living Word, that I might
speak recreating truth to you. I am just
what you always wanted!

"Jesus answered and said to her, 'If you knew the
gift of God, and who it is who says to you, "Give
Me a drink," you would have asked Him, and
He would have given you living water.' "

JOHN 4:10

APRIL
9

JESUS is the

GIVER. All good gifts needed to build up your life and the government of God come from Jesus. He says . . . Open all that I have for you. Use what you received from Me in obedience to My direction. Then My gifts to you will multiply and you will see nations submit to My leadership . . .

"But to each one of us grace was given according to the measure of Christ's gifts. Therefore it says, 'WHEN HE ASCENDED ON HIGH, HE LED CAPTIVE A HOST OF CAPTIVES, AND HE GAVE GIFTS TO MEN.' "

EPHESIANS 4:7–8

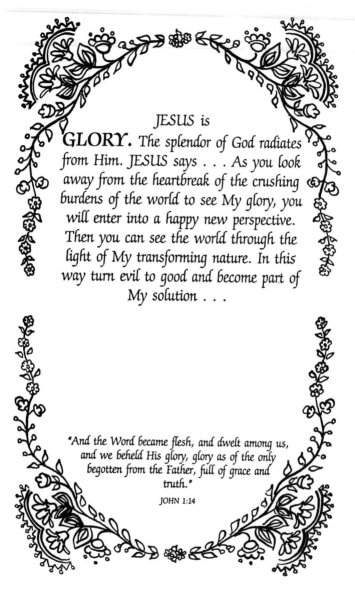

JESUS is

GLORY. The splendor of God radiates from Him. JESUS says . . . As you look away from the heartbreak of the crushing burdens of the world to see My glory, you will enter into a happy new perspective. Then you can see the world through the light of My transforming nature. In this way turn evil to good and become part of My solution . . .

"And the Word became flesh, and dwelt among us, and we beheld His glory, glory as of the only begotten from the Father, full of grace and truth."

JOHN 1:14

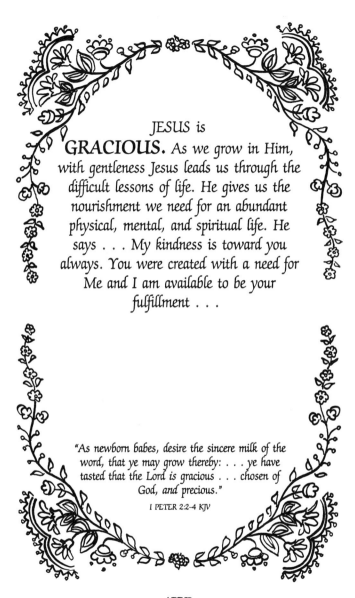

JESUS is
GRACIOUS. As we grow in Him,
with gentleness Jesus leads us through the
difficult lessons of life. He gives us the
nourishment we need for an abundant
physical, mental, and spiritual life. He
says . . . My kindness is toward you
always. You were created with a need for
Me and I am available to be your
fulfillment . . .

"As newborn babes, desire the sincere milk of the
word, that ye may grow thereby: . . . ye have
tasted that the Lord *is* gracious . . . chosen of
God, and precious."

I PETER 2:2–4 KJV

JESUS is
GOD. He makes the claim, either scandalous or true, that He is God come to us in human flesh—fully God yet fully man. Only faith can accept Him. JESUS says . . . Thomas touched My wounds and knew I was who I claimed to be, his Lord and his God. Blessed are you if you believe even when you do not see. When you receive Me, you come into the presence and power of Almighty God . . .

"And He is the image of the invisible God, the firstborn of all creation."
COLOSSIANS 1:15

"I and the Father are one."
JOHN 10:30

JESUS is our
GOVERNOR. He is the One who
has authority to direct the lives and
circumstances of all God's people. He
says . . . My people are in all nations.
Respect the rulers over you. Pray for them
to know Me. Give Me alone the ultimate
power to control your life, for My ways
are not the ways of men. Exercise the
authority you have over others as My
representative . . .

". . . for thus it is written by the prophet, And thou
Bethlehem, in the land of Judah, art not the least
among the princes of Judah: for out of thee
shall come a Governor, that shall rule my
people Israel."

MATTHEW 2:5b,6 KJV

JESUS is the
GLORY of ISRAEL.
He is the light of God that shines through
the history of the Hebrew peoples to
illumine the world. JESUS says . . . God
chose the Jews as His people. I came in
the flesh as a Jewish baby to live and to
freely give up life that all might be able to
come to the living God. As you live in
Me, My glory will shine through you.
Pray that My people, Israel, be drawn to
see Me as the fulfillment of all their law
and hopes . . .

" . . . he took Him into his arms, and blessed God,
and said . . . 'mine eyes have seen Thy salvation,
Which Thou has prepared in the presence of all
peoples, A LIGHT OF REVELATION TO
THE GENTILES, And the glory of Thy
people, Israel.' "
LUKE 2:28,30–32

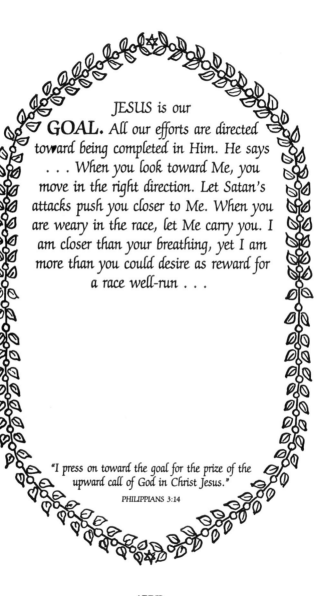

JESUS is our
GOAL. All our efforts are directed toward being completed in Him. He says . . . When you look toward Me, you move in the right direction. Let Satan's attacks push you closer to Me. When you are weary in the race, let Me carry you. I am closer than your breathing, yet I am more than you could desire as reward for a race well-run . . .

"I press on toward the goal for the prize of the upward call of God in Christ Jesus."

PHILIPPIANS 3:14

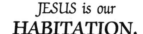

JESUS is our
HABITATION.

He wants us to abide, to live, to stay in
Him. JESUS says . . . As you live in
Me, you will have what you ask. You
will ask what is the perfect will of God,
for your desires will be purified. As you
stay in Me, enduring hardships, your
responses to difficulties will become like
Mine. What a joy!

"Because thou hast made the Lord, *which is my*
refuge, even the most High, thy habitation; There
shall no evil befall thee, neither shall any
plague come nigh thy dwelling."

PSALM 91:9–10 KJV

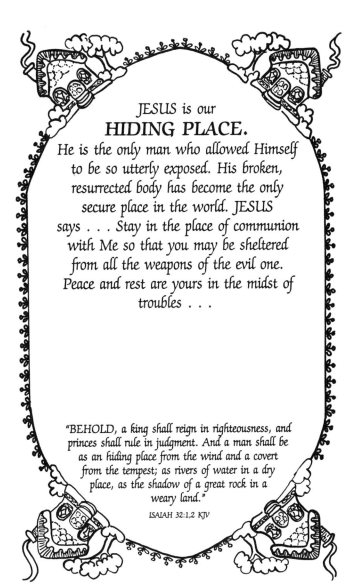

JESUS is our
HIDING PLACE.
He is the only man who allowed Himself
to be so utterly exposed. His broken,
resurrected body has become the only
secure place in the world. JESUS
says . . . Stay in the place of communion
with Me so that you may be sheltered
from all the weapons of the evil one.
Peace and rest are yours in the midst of
troubles . . .

"BEHOLD, a king shall reign in righteousness, and
princes shall rule in judgment. And a man shall be
as an hiding place from the wind and a covert
from the tempest; as rivers of water in a dry
place, as the shadow of a great rock in a
weary land."

ISAIAH 32:1,2 KJV

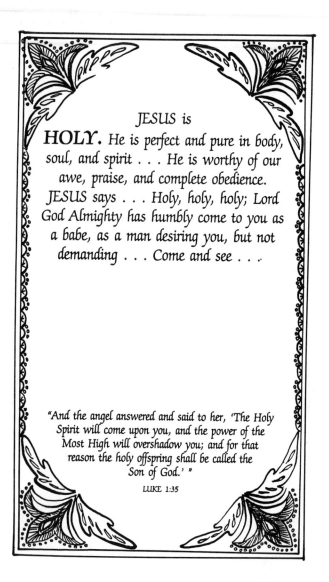

JESUS is
HOLY. He is perfect and pure in body,
soul, and spirit . . . He is worthy of our
awe, praise, and complete obedience.
JESUS says . . . Holy, holy, holy; Lord
God Almighty has humbly come to you as
a babe, as a man desiring you, but not
demanding . . . Come and see . . .

"And the angel answered and said to her, 'The Holy
Spirit will come upon you, and the power of the
Most High will overshadow you; and for that
reason the holy offspring shall be called the
Son of God.' "

LUKE 1:35

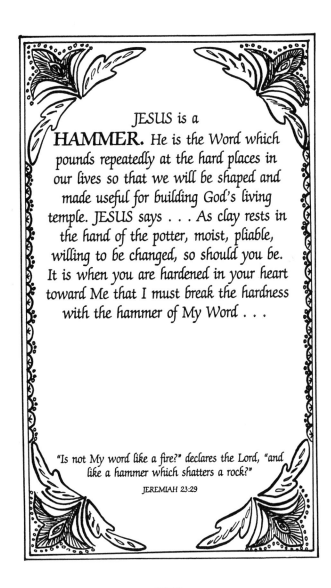

JESUS is a
HAMMER. He is the Word which
pounds repeatedly at the hard places in
our lives so that we will be shaped and
made useful for building God's living
temple. JESUS says . . . As clay rests in
the hand of the potter, moist, pliable,
willing to be changed, so should you be.
It is when you are hardened in your heart
toward Me that I must break the hardness
with the hammer of My Word . . .

"Is not My word like a fire?" declares the Lord, "and
like a hammer which shatters a rock?"

JEREMIAH 23:29

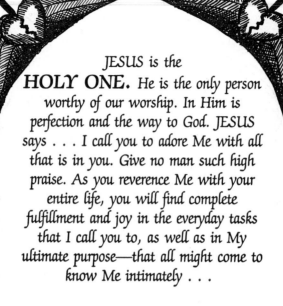

JESUS is the
HOLY ONE. He is the only person
worthy of our worship. In Him is
perfection and the way to God. JESUS
says . . . I call you to adore Me with all
that is in you. Give no man such high
praise. As you reverence Me with your
entire life, you will find complete
fulfillment and joy in the everyday tasks
that I call you to, as well as in My
ultimate purpose—that all might come to
know Me intimately . . .

"But you have an anointing from the Holy One."
I JOHN 2:20

JESUS is
HEARTBROKEN.

On Him was placed all our sin, sickness, and grief. He was despised and rejected. JESUS says . . . My suffering is the door to joyous life for you. As you walk in My steps, you will want to share in My suffering for a lost world, but you will know My victory as well . . .

"Reproach has broken my heart, and I am so sick. And I looked for sympathy, but there was none, And for comforters, but I found none. They also gave me gall for my food, And for my thirst they gave me vinegar to drink."

PSALM 69:20,21

JESUS is our

HUSBAND. He gave His life for us, overcame death, woos us, and is coming for us that we might share His love forever. He says . . . You will be like Me as you spend time with Me and as you lay down your life for others. My delight is to be with you always . . .

"Husbands, love your wives, just as Christ also loved the church and gave Himself up for her; that He might sanctify her, having cleansed her by the washing of water with the word, that He might present to Himself the church in all her glory . . . holy and blameless."

EPHESIANS 5:25–27

JESUS is
HUMBLE.

Although He had all power and prestige available to Him, Jesus left that to become a fragile, vulnerable child of oppressed people. He accepted God's plan for His life, even though that meant death. JESUS says . . . As you deny selfish ambitions and look to God to direct your life, you will find true fulfillment, purpose, and meaning. I will lift you up . . .

"Have this attitude in yourselves which was also in Christ Jesus . . . He humbled Himself by becoming obedient to the point of death . . . on a cross. Therefore also God highly exalted Him, and bestowed on Him the name which is above every name."

PHILIPPIANS 2:5,8b–9

JESUS is our
HEAD. He is the leading member of
the family of God, the authority to which
every Christian bows. JESUS says . . .
Love and kindness are the rods with
which I correct you. I am always alert
and ready to help you. Have this attitude
within the family of God our Father, so
our happiness will overflow into the
world . . .

"And He is before all things, and in Him all things
hold together. He is also head of the body, the
church; and He is the beginning, the firstborn
from the dead; so that He Himself might
come to have first place in everything."

COLOSSIANS 1:17–18

JESUS is the
HIDDEN WISDOM of GOD.
When we get to know Jesus, there are no secrets God withholds from us. God wants us to know His ways and His thoughts which are foolish to the world.

JESUS says . . . Even as a lover whispers delightful things in the ear of His beloved, so let Me be to you. Give My love first place in your life so that I can share with you the depths of God's love . . .

" . . . but we speak God's wisdom in a mystery, the hidden wisdom which God predestined before the ages to our glory; the wisdom which none of the rulers of this age has understood; for if they had understood it, they would not have crucified the Lord of glory."

I CORINTHIANS 2:7–8

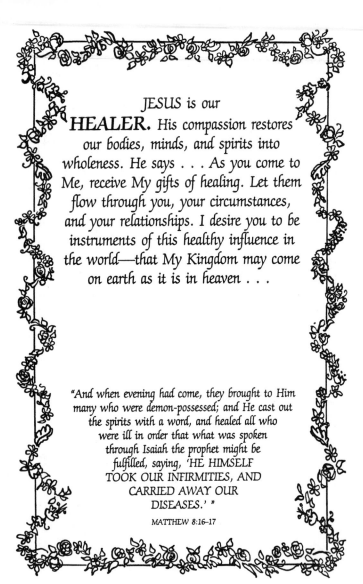

JESUS is our
HEALER. His compassion restores
our bodies, minds, and spirits into
wholeness. He says . . . As you come to
Me, receive My gifts of healing. Let them
flow through you, your circumstances,
and your relationships. I desire you to be
instruments of this healthy influence in
the world—that My Kingdom may come
on earth as it is in heaven . . .

"And when evening had come, they brought to Him
many who were demon-possessed; and He cast out
the spirits with a word, and healed all who
were ill in order that what was spoken
through Isaiah the prophet might be
fulfilled, saying, 'HE HIMSELF
TOOK OUR INFIRMITIES, AND
CARRIED AWAY OUR
DISEASES.' "

MATTHEW 8:16–17

JESUS is our
HOPE. In Him we have unshakable
confidence that God will fulfill all His
promises to us who believe. He says . . .
As you trust Me, I will be in you all
those things which God's joy in you
desires to be. Steadfast endurance, peace,
and love are yours as you boldly come to
Me. And I will complete in you what I
have begun . . .

". . . Christ Jesus, *who* is our hope."

I TIMOTHY 1:1

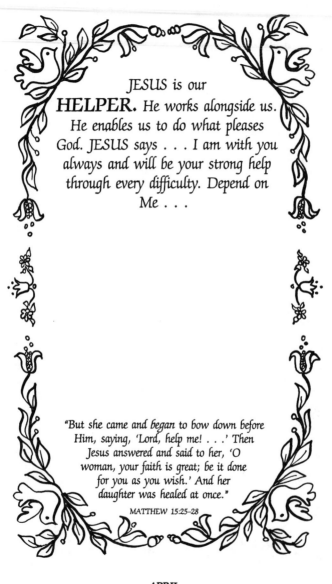

JESUS is our
HELPER. He works alongside us.
He enables us to do what pleases
God. JESUS says . . . I am with you
always and will be your strong help
through every difficulty. Depend on
Me . . .

"But she came and began to bow down before
Him, saying, 'Lord, help me! . . .' Then
Jesus answered and said to her, 'O
woman, your faith is great; be it done
for you as you wish.' And her
daughter was healed at once."

MATTHEW 15:25–28

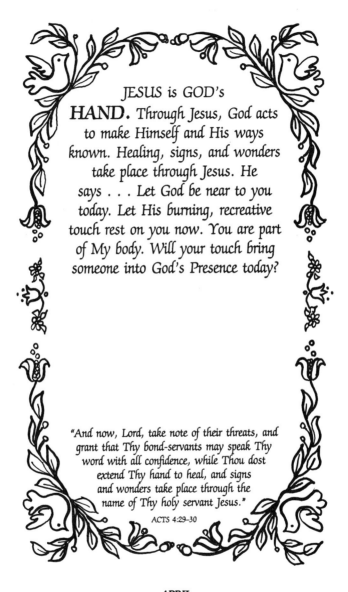

JESUS is GOD's **HAND.** Through Jesus, God acts to make Himself and His ways known. Healing, signs, and wonders take place through Jesus. He says . . . Let God be near to you today. Let His burning, recreative touch rest on you now. You are part of My body. Will your touch bring someone into God's Presence today?

"And now, Lord, take note of their threats, and grant that Thy bond-servants may speak Thy word with all confidence, while Thou dost extend Thy hand to heal, and signs and wonders take place through the name of Thy holy servant Jesus."

ACTS 4:29–30

APRIL
30

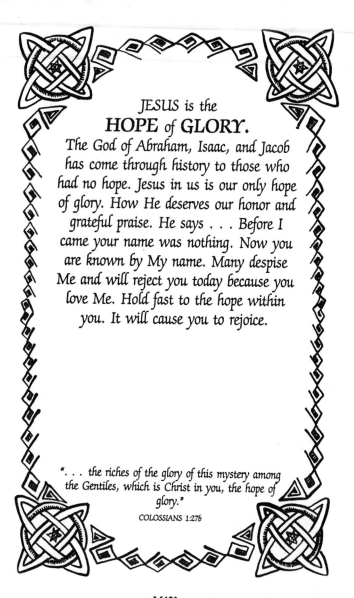

JESUS is the
HOPE of GLORY.

The God of Abraham, Isaac, and Jacob
has come through history to those who
had no hope. Jesus in us is our only hope
of glory. How He deserves our honor and
grateful praise. He says . . . Before I
came your name was nothing. Now you
are known by My name. Many despise
Me and will reject you today because you
love Me. Hold fast to the hope within
you. It will cause you to rejoice.

". . . the riches of the glory of this mystery among
the Gentiles, which is Christ in you, the hope of
glory."

COLOSSIANS 1:27b

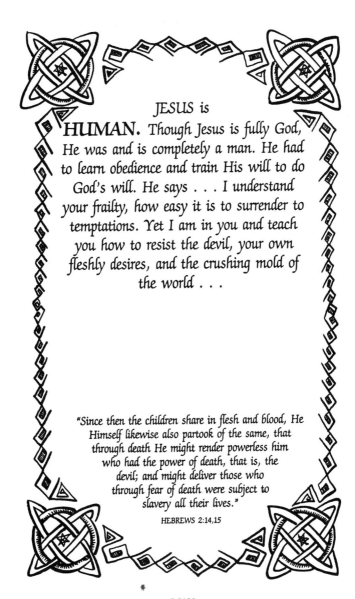

JESUS is

HUMAN. Though Jesus is fully God, He was and is completely a man. He had to learn obedience and train His will to do God's will. He says . . . I understand your frailty, how easy it is to surrender to temptations. Yet I am in you and teach you how to resist the devil, your own fleshly desires, and the crushing mold of the world . . .

"Since then the children share in flesh and blood, He Himself likewise also partook of the same, that through death He might render powerless him who had the power of death, that is, the devil; and might deliver those who through fear of death were subject to slavery all their lives."

HEBREWS 2:14,15

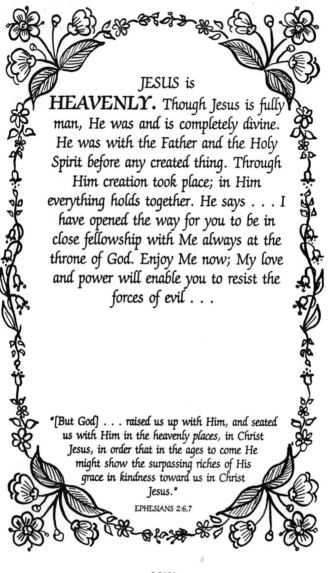

JESUS is
HEAVENLY. Though Jesus is fully man, He was and is completely divine. He was with the Father and the Holy Spirit before any created thing. Through Him creation took place; in Him everything holds together. He says . . . I have opened the way for you to be in close fellowship with Me always at the throne of God. Enjoy Me now; My love and power will enable you to resist the forces of evil . . .

"[But God] . . . raised us up with Him, and seated us with Him in the heavenly places, in Christ Jesus, in order that in the ages to come He might show the surpassing riches of His grace in kindness toward us in Christ Jesus."

EPHESIANS 2:6,7

JESUS is the
HEADSTONE. He is the living
memorial to all God has done in the past
and the foundation of all He will do.
JESUS says . . . Build on Me. Become
fulfilled and complete in Me, or refuse Me
and all your efforts will fall . . .

"The stone *which* the builders refused is become the
head *stone* of the corner. This is the LORD'S
doing; *it is* marvelous in our eyes."

PSALM 118:22–23 KJV

MAY
4

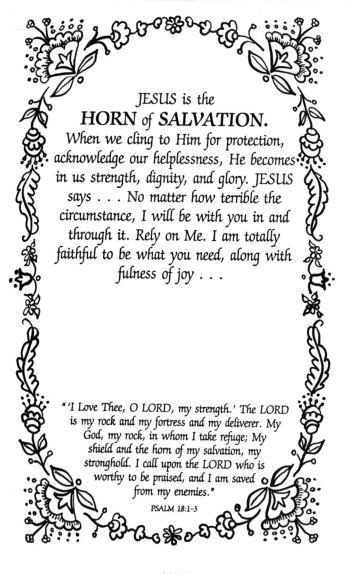

JESUS is the
HORN of SALVATION.
When we cling to Him for protection,
acknowledge our helplessness, He becomes
in us strength, dignity, and glory. JESUS
says . . . No matter how terrible the
circumstance, I will be with you in and
through it. Rely on Me. I am totally
faithful to be what you need, along with
fulness of joy . . .

" 'I Love Thee, O LORD, my strength.' The LORD
is my rock and my fortress and my deliverer. My
God, my rock, in whom I take refuge; My
shield and the horn of my salvation, my
stronghold. I call upon the LORD who is
worthy to be praised, and I am saved
from my enemies."

PSALM 18:1–3

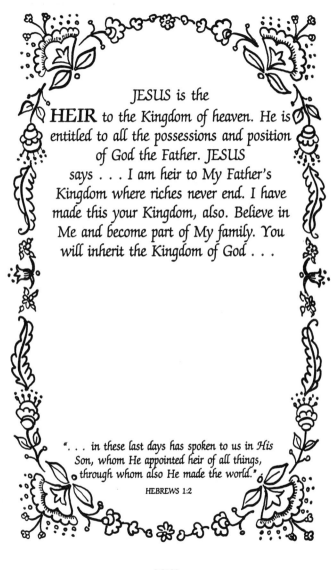

JESUS is the **HEIR** to the Kingdom of heaven. He is entitled to all the possessions and position of God the Father. JESUS says . . . I am heir to My Father's Kingdom where riches never end. I have made this your Kingdom, also. Believe in Me and become part of My family. You will inherit the Kingdom of God . . .

". . . in these last days has spoken to us in His Son, whom He appointed heir of all things, through whom also He made the world."

HEBREWS 1:2

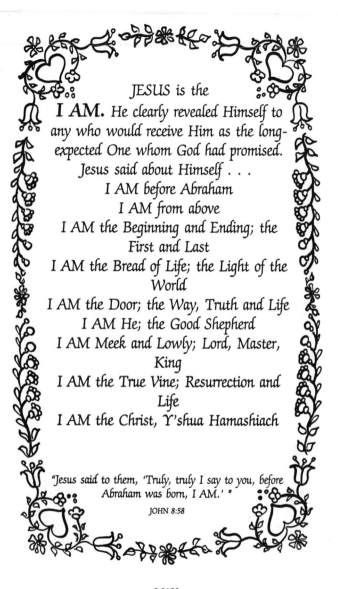

JESUS is the
I AM. He clearly revealed Himself to any who would receive Him as the long-expected One whom God had promised. Jesus said about Himself . . .

I AM before Abraham

I AM from above

I AM the Beginning and Ending; the First and Last

I AM the Bread of Life; the Light of the World

I AM the Door; the Way, Truth and Life

I AM He; the Good Shepherd

I AM Meek and Lowly; Lord, Master, King

I AM the True Vine; Resurrection and Life

I AM the Christ, Y'shua Hamashiach

"Jesus said to them, 'Truly, truly I say to you, before Abraham was born, I AM.' "

JOHN 8:58

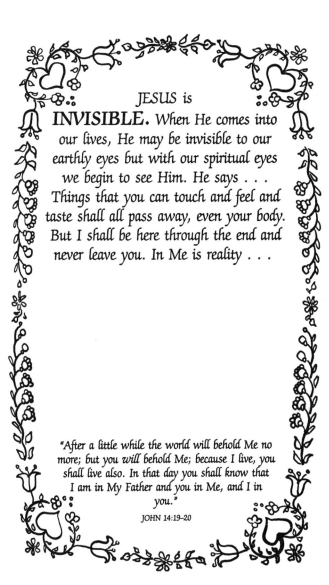

JESUS is
INVISIBLE. When He comes into
our lives, He may be invisible to our
earthly eyes but with our spiritual eyes
we begin to see Him. He says . . .
Things that you can touch and feel and
taste shall all pass away, even your body.
But I shall be here through the end and
never leave you. In Me is reality . . .

"After a little while the world will behold Me no
more; but you *will* behold Me; because I live, you
shall live also. In that day you shall know that
I am in My Father and you in Me, and I in
you."

JOHN 14:19–20

JESUS is our
INSTRUCTOR.
He is our teacher in the things of God.
JESUS says . . . Fill your mind with
things which will edify, build you up in
Me. Let My Holy Spirit open up the
Word of God to you. Allow Me to erase
those images from your mind which you
allowed the world to draw there. The
pictures I form in you are true, honorable,
right, pure, lovely, of good repute,
excellent and worthy of praise. Think
about them . . .

"But he who is spiritual appraises all things, yet he
himself is appraised by no man. For WHO HAS
KNOWN THE MIND OF THE LORD,
THAT HE SHOULD INSTRUCT HIM?
But we have the mind of Christ."

I CORINTHIANS 2:15–16

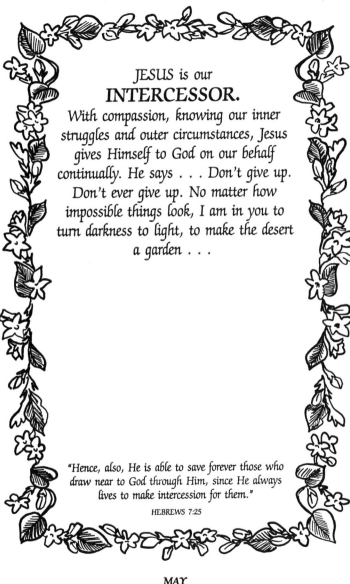

JESUS is our
INTERCESSOR.

With compassion, knowing our inner
struggles and outer circumstances, Jesus
gives Himself to God on our behalf
continually. He says . . . Don't give up.
Don't ever give up. No matter how
impossible things look, I am in you to
turn darkness to light, to make the desert
a garden . . .

"Hence, also, He is able to save forever those who
draw near to God through Him, since He always
lives to make intercession for them."

HEBREWS 7:25

JESUS is
IMMANUEL.

The angel told Joseph that Jesus would be
"God with us," Immanuel. JESUS
says . . . I am with you always, even to
the close of the age. Whatever the
darkness or difficulty, I will take you
through . . .

" 'BEHOLD, THE VIRGIN SHALL BE WITH
CHILD, AND SHALL BEAR A SON AND
THEY SHALL CALL HIS NAME
IMMANUEL,' which translated means
'GOD WITH US.' "

MATTHEW 1:23

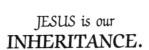

JESUS is our
INHERITANCE.

He is our salvation, abundant life now,
and our eternal life after death. He
says . . . Have you left anything or
anyone because you love Me? Has it cost
you anything to follow Me? I have
promised this back to you one hundredfold
and all that I have eternally with our
Father, the Almighty God . . .

"Blessed be the God and Father of our Lord Jesus
Christ, who according to His great mercy has
caused us to be born again to a living hope
through the resurrection of Jesus Christ from
the dead, to obtain an inheritance which
is imperishable and . . . will not fade
away, reserved in heaven for you."

I PETER 1:3–4

JESUS is our
IMMORTALITY.

In Him our abundant life here is just the beginning, a taste of the imperishable life to come. JESUS says . . . Dare to live fully now. In a world darkened by evil look for My light. You will find Me. Let your body be energized with My Spirit, empowered to be a shining witness so that you will know life now and forever is joy . . .

". . . join with me in suffering for the gospel according to the power of God, who . . . saved us . . . according to His own purpose and grace which was granted us in Christ Jesus from all eternity, but now has been revealed by the appearing of our Savior Christ Jesus, who abolished death, and brought life and immortality to light through the gospel."

II TIMOTHY 1:8b–10

JESUS is the
IMAGE of **GOD.** He is "the
reflection of eternal light," "a spotless
mirror of the working of God," "the image
of His goodness" (WISDOM of Solomon
7:25–26). JESUS says . . . You were
created to be the image of God. With My
life in you, you, too, reflect who God is
as long as you keep turned towards Him.
You will shine as you meet Him face-to-
face . . .

"And He is the image of the invisible God, the first-
born of all creation."

COLOSSIANS 1:15

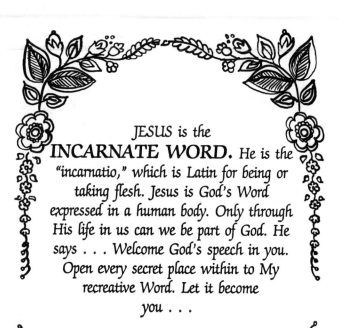

JESUS is the
INCARNATE WORD. He is the
"incarnatio," which is Latin for being or
taking flesh. Jesus is God's Word
expressed in a human body. Only through
His life in us can we be part of God. He
says . . . Welcome God's speech in you.
Open every secret place within to My
recreative Word. Let it become
you . . .

"And the Word became flesh, and dwelt among us,
and we beheld His glory, glory as of the only
begotten from the Father, full of grace and
truth."

JOHN 1:14

MAY
15

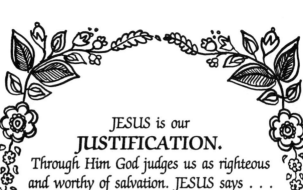

JESUS is our
JUSTIFICATION.
Through Him God judges us as righteous
and worthy of salvation. JESUS says . . .
Stop trying to justify yourself. Let your
actions, thoughts, and motives be brought
before the cleansing fire of My Presence.
The wounds, the death they deserve have
been paid. Humble yourself so that I may
exalt you . . .

". . . those who receive the abundance of grace and
of the gift of righteousness will reign in life
through the One, Jesus Christ . . . through one
act of righteousness there resulted
justification of life to all men."

ROMANS 5:17b,18b

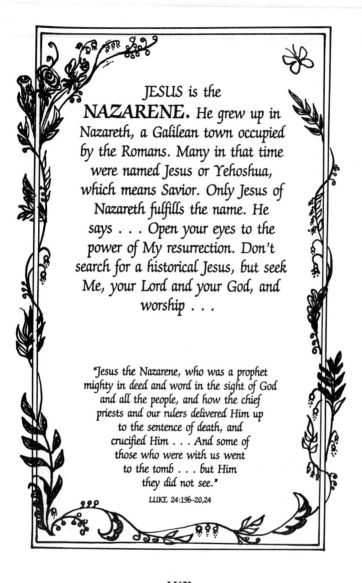

JESUS is the
NAZARENE. He grew up in
Nazareth, a Galilean town occupied
by the Romans. Many in that time
were named Jesus or Yehoshua,
which means Savior. Only Jesus of
Nazareth fulfills the name. He
says . . . Open your eyes to the
power of My resurrection. Don't
search for a historical Jesus, but seek
Me, your Lord and your God, and
worship . . .

"Jesus the Nazarene, who was a prophet
mighty in deed and word in the sight of God
and all the people, and how the chief
priests and our rulers delivered Him up
to the sentence of death, and
crucified Him . . . And some of
those who were with us went
to the tomb . . . but Him
they did not see."

LUKE 24:19b–20,24

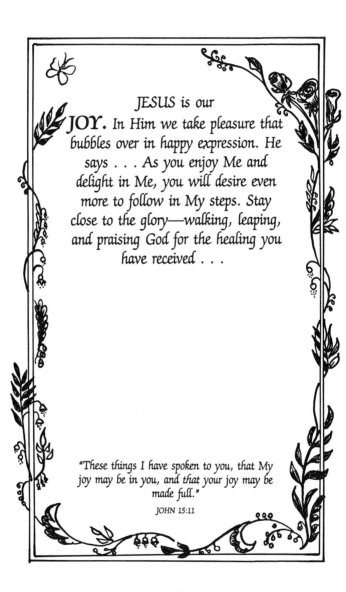

JESUS is our

JOY. In Him we take pleasure that bubbles over in happy expression. He says . . . As you enjoy Me and delight in Me, you will desire even more to follow in My steps. Stay close to the glory—walking, leaping, and praising God for the healing you have received . . .

"These things I have spoken to you, that My joy may be in you, and that your joy may be made full."

JOHN 15:11

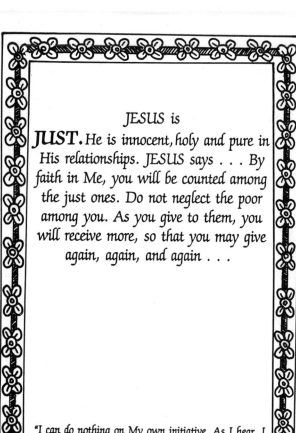

JESUS is
JUST. He is innocent, holy and pure in His relationships. JESUS says . . . By faith in Me, you will be counted among the just ones. Do not neglect the poor among you. As you give to them, you will receive more, so that you may give again, again, and again . . .

"I can do nothing on My own initiative. As I hear, I judge; and My judgment is just, because I do not seek My own will, but the will of Him who sent Me."

JOHN 5:30

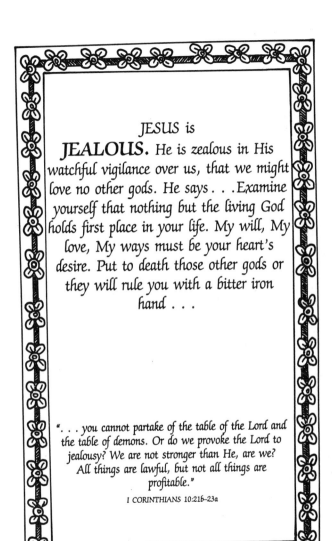

JESUS is

JEALOUS. He is zealous in His watchful vigilance over us, that we might love no other gods. He says . . . Examine yourself that nothing but the living God holds first place in your life. My will, My love, My ways must be your heart's desire. Put to death those other gods or they will rule you with a bitter iron hand . . .

" . . . you cannot partake of the table of the Lord and the table of demons. Or do we provoke the Lord to jealousy? We are not stronger than He, are we? All things are lawful, but not all things are profitable."

I CORINTHIANS 10:21b–23a

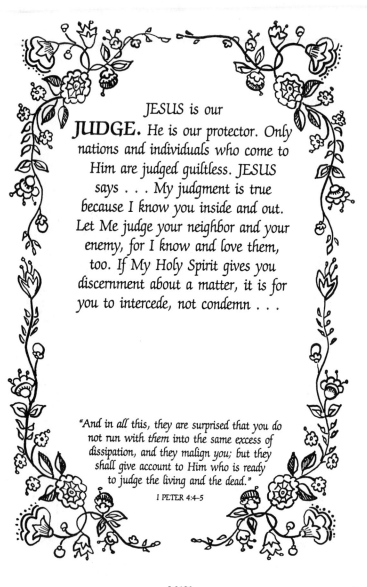

JESUS is our **JUDGE.** He is our protector. Only nations and individuals who come to Him are judged guiltless. JESUS says . . . My judgment is true because I know you inside and out. Let Me judge your neighbor and your enemy, for I know and love them, too. If My Holy Spirit gives you discernment about a matter, it is for you to intercede, not condemn . . .

"And in all this, they are surprised that you do not run with them into the same excess of dissipation, and they malign you; but they shall give account to Him who is ready to judge the living and the dead."

I PETER 4:4-5

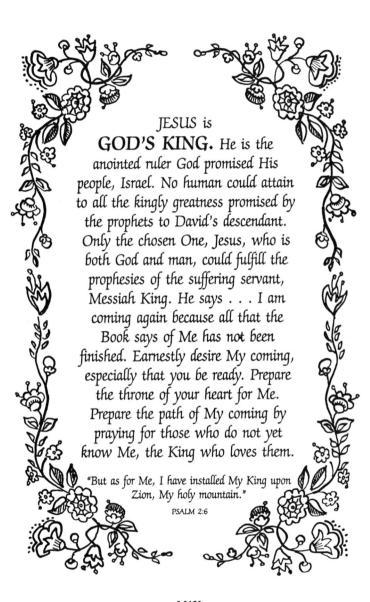

JESUS is
GOD'S KING. He is the
anointed ruler God promised His
people, Israel. No human could attain
to all the kingly greatness promised by
the prophets to David's descendant.
Only the chosen One, Jesus, who is
both God and man, could fulfill the
prophesies of the suffering servant,
Messiah King. He says . . . I am
coming again because all that the
Book says of Me has not been
finished. Earnestly desire My coming,
especially that you be ready. Prepare
the throne of your heart for Me.
Prepare the path of My coming by
praying for those who do not yet
know Me, the King who loves them.

"But as for Me, I have installed My King upon
Zion, My holy mountain."

PSALM 2:6

JESUS is our
KINSMAN REDEEMER.

Through the love and compassion of Boaz, Naomi, the desolate widow, and Ruth, the despised Moabitess, were rescued and restored. Jesus came from that union and is our Kinsman Redeemer. He marries the despised Gentiles who come humbly to Him and He gladdens the heart of all the desolate of Israel who look to Him. He says . . . My love burns and the creation groans in travail until both Jew and Gentile come into My bridal chamber. How I long to express My love to My own people, the Jews. Pray that My love for them be expressed through you . . .

"Then the women said to Naomi, 'Blessed is the Lord who has not left you without a redeemer today, and may his name become famous in Israel.' "

RUTH 4:14

JESUS is

KEEPER. He watches day and night to guard us from injury. JESUS says . . . All over the world your brothers and sisters are being starved, tortured, and tormented when their only crime is that they love Me and will not deny My name. In the midst of suffering, I keep them. Resist fear for your own safety. Ask, "What can I do to help the poor and persecuted with the resources God has given me?"

"Because you have kept the word of My perseverance, I also will keep you from the hour of testing, that hour which is about to come upon the whole world, to test those who dwell upon the earth. I am coming quickly; hold fast."

REVELATION 3:10–11a

JESUS has the

KEY. He enables us to gain entrance to the shekinah glory of God's Presence. With Him, we can storm the places where Satan holds people prisoner and open the door of life for them. JESUS says . . . I wait for you to ask so that My will can be done—to preach Good News to the poor, heal the brokenhearted, announce that captives and downtrodden shall be freed, and that the blind shall see. God wants to give His blessings through you . . .

"I will give you the keys of the kingdom of heaven; and whatever you shall bind on earth shall have been bound in heaven, and whatever you shall loose on earth shall have been loosed in heaven."

MATTHEW 16:19

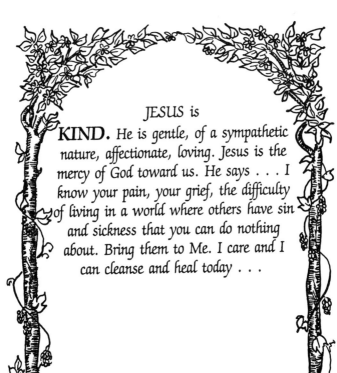

JESUS is

KIND. He is gentle, of a sympathetic nature, affectionate, loving. Jesus is the mercy of God toward us. He says . . . I know your pain, your grief, the difficulty of living in a world where others have sin and sickness that you can do nothing about. Bring them to Me. I care and I can cleanse and heal today . . .

" . . . raised us up with Him, and seated us with Him in the heavenly places, in Christ Jesus, in order that in the ages to come He might show the surpassing riches of his grace in kindness toward us in Christ Jesus."

EPHESIANS 2:6–7

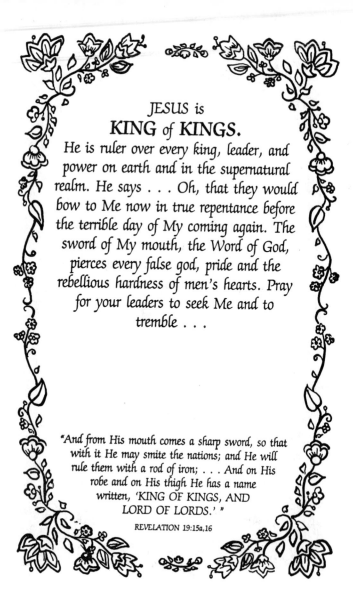

JESUS is
KING of **KINGS.**

He is ruler over every king, leader, and power on earth and in the supernatural realm. He says . . . Oh, that they would bow to Me now in true repentance before the terrible day of My coming again. The sword of My mouth, the Word of God, pierces every false god, pride and the rebellious hardness of men's hearts. Pray for your leaders to seek Me and to tremble . . .

"And from His mouth comes a sharp sword, so that with it He may smite the nations; and He will rule them with a rod of iron; . . . And on His robe and on His thigh He has a name written, 'KING OF KINGS, AND LORD OF LORDS.' "

REVELATION 19:15a,16

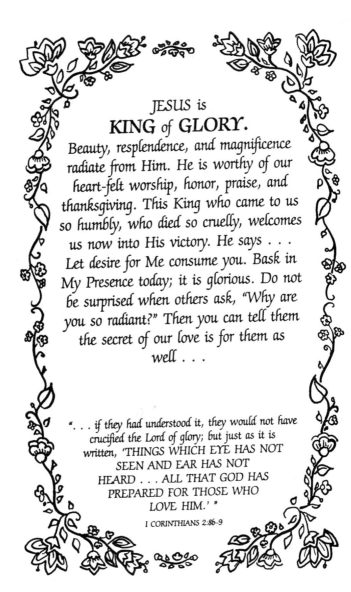

JESUS is
KING of GLORY.

Beauty, resplendence, and magnificence radiate from Him. He is worthy of our heart-felt worship, honor, praise, and thanksgiving. This King who came to us so humbly, who died so cruelly, welcomes us now into His victory. He says . . . Let desire for Me consume you. Bask in My Presence today; it is glorious. Do not be surprised when others ask, "Why are you so radiant?" Then you can tell them the secret of our love is for them as well . . .

" . . . if they had understood it, they would not have crucified the Lord of glory; but just as it is written, 'THINGS WHICH EYE HAS NOT SEEN AND EAR HAS NOT HEARD . . . ALL THAT GOD HAS PREPARED FOR THOSE WHO LOVE HIM.' "

I CORINTHIANS 2:8b–9

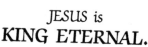

JESUS is
KING ETERNAL.

He is reigning now, seated on the throne at the right hand of God, ONE with God forever. Every power and ruler of darkness, visible and invisible, trembles under His feet. JESUS says . . . Take your position with Me. Put all the ugly attitudes to death quickly; they cannot rest here with Me in the beauty of holiness. Take authority over the evil you see around you. I need My disciples to speak the word of faith to the forces which have caught My little ones in traps of darkness. Let your light shine!

"Now to the King eternal, immortal, invisible, the only God, be honor and glory forever and ever. Amen."

I TIMOTHY 1:17

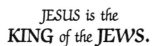

JESUS is the
KING of the **JEWS.**

He is the long-expected Messianic King of
Israel. JESUS says . . . Oh, how I yearn
for My beloved people, the Jews, to
recognize that I am the King God sent
them. Then their mourning would turn to
dancing, the oil of gladness would spill
over them. Seek out My people, the Jews,
and love them with My love. Pray for
them with My tears. Receive them with
My joy—for in Me the promise of their
heritage is fulfilled . . .

"And Pilate questioned Him, 'Are You the King of
the Jews?' And answering He said to him, 'It *is*
as you say.' "

MARK 15:2

JESUS is the
LAMB of **GOD.** He, the only
perfect innocent One, allowed Himself
to be helpless, to be taken out to the
garbage dump and cruelly killed so that
through receiving the sacrifice of His life's
blood we could be cleansed before God.
JESUS says . . . Freely My blood poured
out for you. Cover yourself with it so that
the trusting, innocent nature of the Lamb
of God will replace your old, rotten
nature. As you stand in the stream of My
forgiveness, you will find it a joy to
forgive others . . .

" . . . conduct yourselves in fear during the time of
your stay upon earth; knowing that you were . . .
redeemed . . . with precious blood, as of a lamb
unblemished . . . the blood of Christ."

I PETER 1:17b–19

JESUS is
LORD of LORDS.
No authority on earth or in the spiritual realm is greater than the power of our Lord Jesus. He says . . . Nations come and go, but I remain King of Kings and Lord of Lords. Let My throne be in your heart always . . .

"And from His mouth comes a sharp sword, so that with it He may smite the nations; and He will rule them with a rod of iron; . . . And on His robe and on His thigh He has a name written, 'KING OF KINGS, AND LORD OF LORDS.' "

REVELATION 19:15a–16

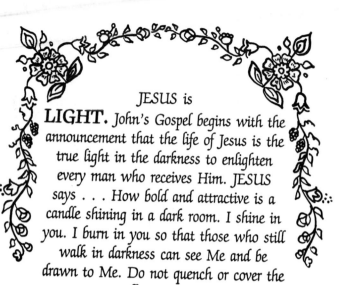

JESUS is
LIGHT. John's Gospel begins with the announcement that the life of Jesus is the true light in the darkness to enlighten every man who receives Him. JESUS says . . . How bold and attractive is a candle shining in a dark room. I shine in you. I burn in you so that those who still walk in darkness can see Me and be drawn to Me. Do not quench or cover the flame . . .

" . . . Jesus spoke to them, saying, 'I am the light of the world; he who follows Me shall not walk in the darkness, but shall have the light of life.' "

JOHN 8:12

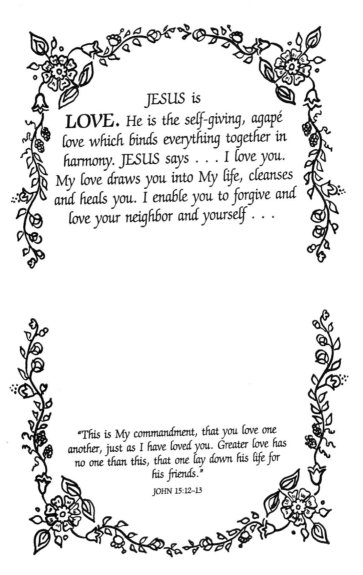

JESUS is
LOVE. He is the self-giving, agapé love which binds everything together in harmony. JESUS says . . . I love you. My love draws you into My life, cleanses and heals you. I enable you to forgive and love your neighbor and yourself . . .

"This is My commandment, that you love one another, just as I have loved you. Greater love has no one than this, that one lay down his life for his friends."

JOHN 15:12–13

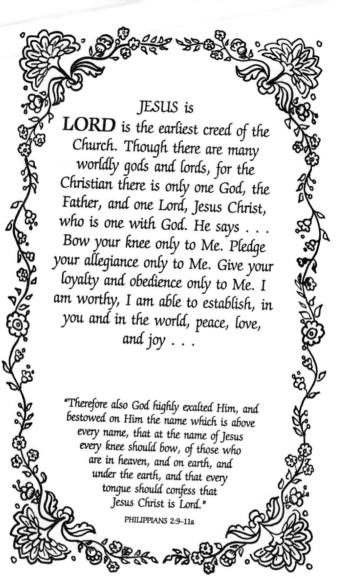

JESUS is
LORD is the earliest creed of the Church. Though there are many worldly gods and lords, for the Christian there is only one God, the Father, and one Lord, Jesus Christ, who is one with God. He says . . . Bow your knee only to Me. Pledge your allegiance only to Me. Give your loyalty and obedience only to Me. I am worthy, I am able to establish, in you and in the world, peace, love, and joy . . .

"Therefore also God highly exalted Him, and bestowed on Him the name which is above every name, that at the name of Jesus every knee should bow, of those who are in heaven, and on earth, and under the earth, and that every tongue should confess that Jesus Christ is Lord."

PHILIPPIANS 2:9–11a

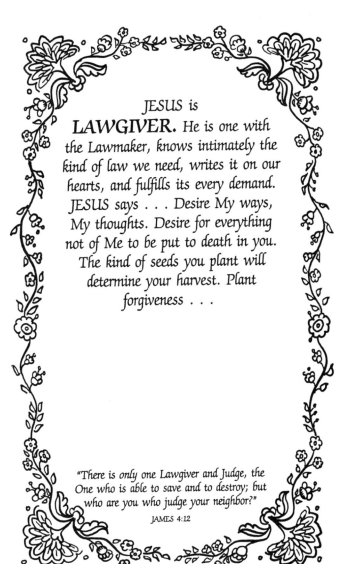

JESUS is
LAWGIVER. He is one with
the Lawmaker, knows intimately the
kind of law we need, writes it on our
hearts, and fulfills its every demand.
JESUS says . . . Desire My ways,
My thoughts. Desire for everything
not of Me to be put to death in you.
The kind of seeds you plant will
determine your harvest. Plant
forgiveness . . .

"There is only one Lawgiver and Judge, the
One who is able to save and to destroy; but
who are you who judge your neighbor?"

JAMES 4:12

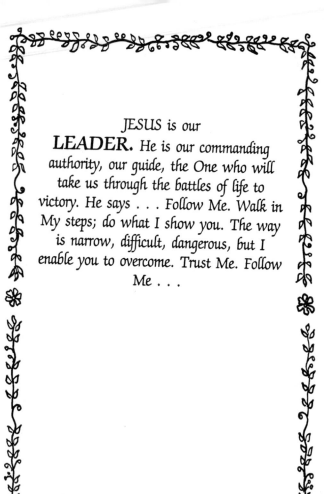

JESUS is our
LEADER. He is our commanding
authority, our guide, the One who will
take us through the battles of life to
victory. He says . . . Follow Me. Walk in
My steps; do what I show you. The way
is narrow, difficult, dangerous, but I
enable you to overcome. Trust Me. Follow
Me . . .

"Behold, I have made him a witness to the peoples.
A leader and commander for the peoples."

ISAIAH 55:4

JESUS is
LORD of the **SABBATH.**
He is the One who shows us how best to
order our lives to worship God, and how
to enter into rest. He is the fulfillment of
the fourth law of Moses. JESUS
says . . . Come to Me and rest. Let My
Presence refresh you and enable you to
live in such a way that you are free to
truly give of yourself to those in need as I
direct you . . .

"But if you had known what this means 'I DESIRE
COMPASSION, AND NOT A SACRIFICE,'
you would not have condemned the innocent.
For the Son of Man is Lord of the Sabbath."

MATTHEW 12:7–8

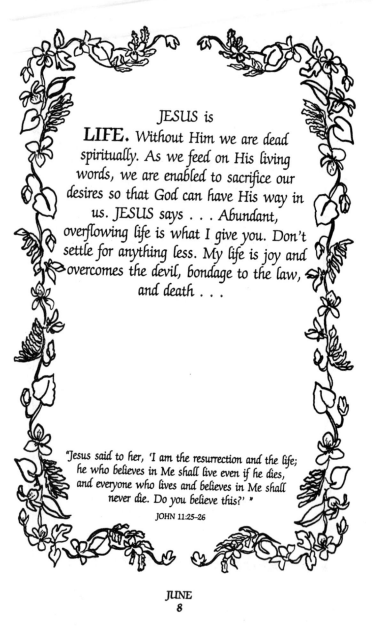

JESUS is
LIFE. Without Him we are dead spiritually. As we feed on His living words, we are enabled to sacrifice our desires so that God can have His way in us. JESUS says . . . Abundant, overflowing life is what I give you. Don't settle for anything less. My life is joy and overcomes the devil, bondage to the law, and death . . .

"Jesus said to her, 'I am the resurrection and the life; he who believes in Me shall live even if he dies, and everyone who lives and believes in Me shall never die. Do you believe this?' "

JOHN 11:25–26

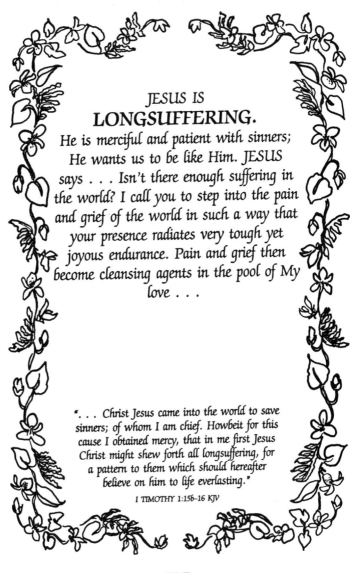

JESUS IS
LONGSUFFERING.

He is merciful and patient with sinners;
He wants us to be like Him. JESUS
says . . . Isn't there enough suffering in
the world? I call you to step into the pain
and grief of the world in such a way that
your presence radiates very tough yet
joyous endurance. Pain and grief then
become cleansing agents in the pool of My
love . . .

"... Christ Jesus came into the world to save
sinners; of whom I am chief. Howbeit for this
cause I obtained mercy, that in me first Jesus
Christ might shew forth all longsuffering, for
a pattern to them which should hereafter
believe on him to life everlasting."

I TIMOTHY 1:15b–16 KJV

JESUS is
LOWLY. He is free from pride; He says and does only what the Father God shows Him. JESUS says . . . My obedience led Me where I did not want to go—yet aren't you glad I was willing? Let Me show you the Father's will for you. Walk in it. Even though it costs your life, it is the place of perfect peace . . .

"Come unto Me, all ye that labour and are heavy laden, and I will give you rest. Take my yoke upon you, and learn of me; for I am meek and lowly in heart: and ye shall find rest unto your souls. For my yoke is easy, and my burden is light."

MATTHEW 11:28–30 KJV

JESUS is the
LORD JESUS. His is the authority deserving of our joyful obedience because He gave Himself for us. JESUS says . . . What within you dictates what you do, even though you don't want to do that wrong thing? I tell you, love Me more than these; depose the dictators in your heart. Let My Spirit have His way in you . . .

"And whatever you do in word or deed, do all in the name of the Lord Jesus, giving thanks through Him to God the Father."

COLOSSIANS 3:17

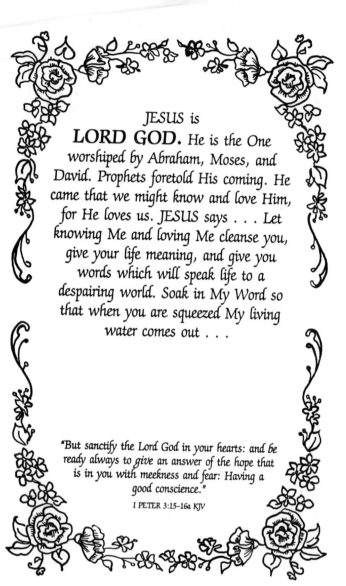

JESUS is
LORD GOD. He is the One
worshiped by Abraham, Moses, and
David. Prophets foretold His coming. He
came that we might know and love Him,
for He loves us. JESUS says . . . Let
knowing Me and loving Me cleanse you,
give your life meaning, and give you
words which will speak life to a
despairing world. Soak in My Word so
that when you are squeezed My living
water comes out . . .

"But sanctify the Lord God in your hearts: and be
ready always to *give* an answer of the hope that
is in you with meekness and fear: Having a
good conscience."

I PETER 3:15–16a KJV

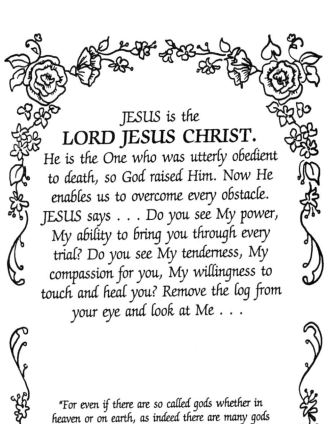

JESUS is the
LORD JESUS CHRIST.
He is the One who was utterly obedient
to death, so God raised Him. Now He
enables us to overcome every obstacle.
JESUS says . . . Do you see My power,
My ability to bring you through every
trial? Do you see My tenderness, My
compassion for you, My willingness to
touch and heal you? Remove the log from
your eye and look at Me . . .

"For even if there are so called gods whether in
heaven or on earth, as indeed there are many gods
and many lords, yet for us there is but one
God, the Father, from whom are all things,
and we exist for Him; and one Lord,
Jesus Christ, through whom are all
things, and we exist through Him."

I CORINTHIANS 8:5,6

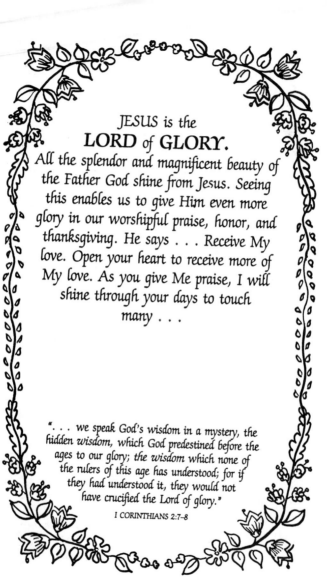

JESUS is the
LORD of GLORY.

All the splendor and magnificent beauty of the Father God shine from Jesus. Seeing this enables us to give Him even more glory in our worshipful praise, honor, and thanksgiving. He says . . . Receive My love. Open your heart to receive more of My love. As you give Me praise, I will shine through your days to touch many . . .

" . . . we speak God's wisdom in a mystery, the hidden *wisdom*, which God predestined before the ages to our glory; *the wisdom* which none of the rulers of this age has understood; for if they had understood it, they would not have crucified the Lord of glory."

I CORINTHIANS 2:7–8

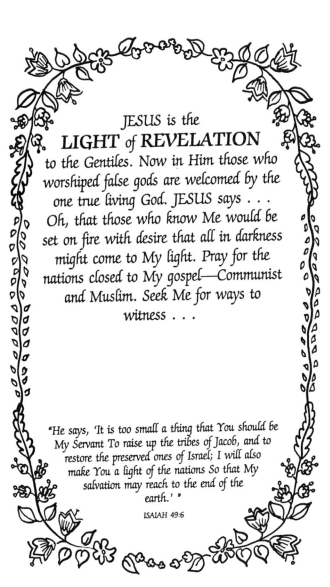

JESUS is the
LIGHT of REVELATION

to the Gentiles. Now in Him those who
worshiped false gods are welcomed by the
one true living God. JESUS says . . .
Oh, that those who know Me would be
set on fire with desire that all in darkness
might come to My light. Pray for the
nations closed to My gospel—Communist
and Muslim. Seek Me for ways to
witness . . .

"He says, 'It is too small a thing that You should be
My Servant To raise up the tribes of Jacob, and to
restore the preserved ones of Israel; I will also
make You a light of the nations So that My
salvation may reach to the end of the
earth.' "

ISAIAH 49:6

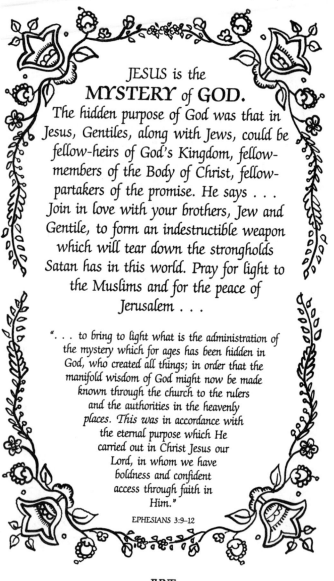

JESUS is the
MYSTERY of GOD.

The hidden purpose of God was that in
Jesus, Gentiles, along with Jews, could be
fellow-heirs of God's Kingdom, fellow-
members of the Body of Christ, fellow-
partakers of the promise. He says . . .
Join in love with your brothers, Jew and
Gentile, to form an indestructible weapon
which will tear down the strongholds
Satan has in this world. Pray for light to
the Muslims and for the peace of
Jerusalem . . .

" . . . to bring to light what is the administration of
the mystery which for ages has been hidden in
God, who created all things; in order that the
manifold wisdom of God might now be made
known through the church to the rulers
and the authorities in the heavenly
places. This was in accordance with
the eternal purpose which He
carried out in Christ Jesus our
Lord, in whom we have
boldness and confident
access through faith in
Him."

EPHESIANS 3:9–12

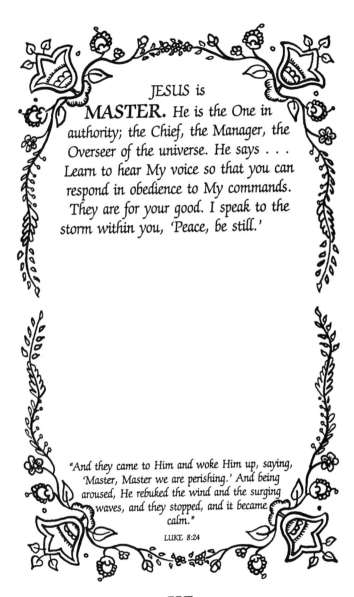

JESUS is

MASTER. He is the One in authority; the Chief, the Manager, the Overseer of the universe. He says . . . Learn to hear My voice so that you can respond in obedience to My commands. They are for your good. I speak to the storm within you, 'Peace, be still.'

"And they came to Him and woke Him up, saying, 'Master, Master we are perishing.' And being aroused, He rebuked the wind and the surging waves, and they stopped, and it became calm."

LUKE 8:24

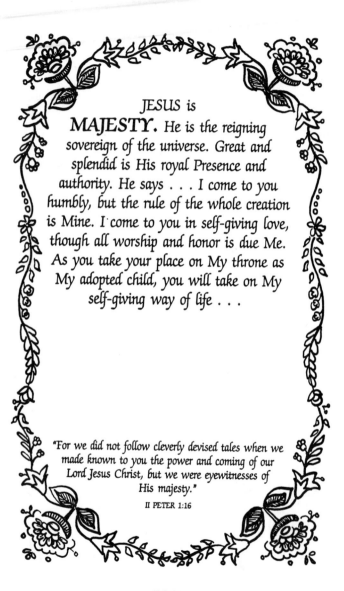

JESUS is **MAJESTY.** He is the reigning sovereign of the universe. Great and splendid is His royal Presence and authority. He says . . . I come to you humbly, but the rule of the whole creation is Mine. I come to you in self-giving love, though all worship and honor is due Me. As you take your place on My throne as My adopted child, you will take on My self-giving way of life . . .

"For we did not follow cleverly devised tales when we made known to you the power and coming of our Lord Jesus Christ, but we were eyewitnesses of His majesty."

II PETER 1:16

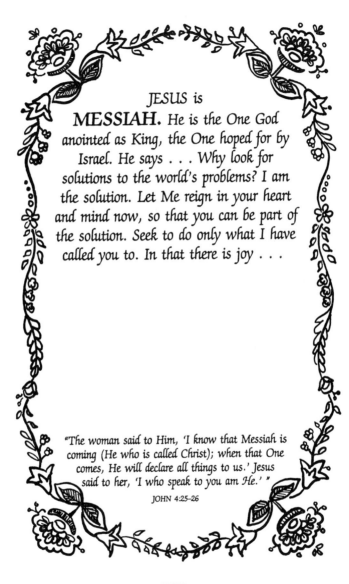

JESUS is
MESSIAH. He is the One God
anointed as King, the One hoped for by
Israel. He says . . . Why look for
solutions to the world's problems? I am
the solution. Let Me reign in your heart
and mind now, so that you can be part of
the solution. Seek to do only what I have
called you to. In that there is joy . . .

"The woman said to Him, 'I know that Messiah is
coming (He who is called Christ); when that One
comes, He will declare all things to us.' Jesus
said to her, 'I who speak to you am He.' "

JOHN 4:25–26

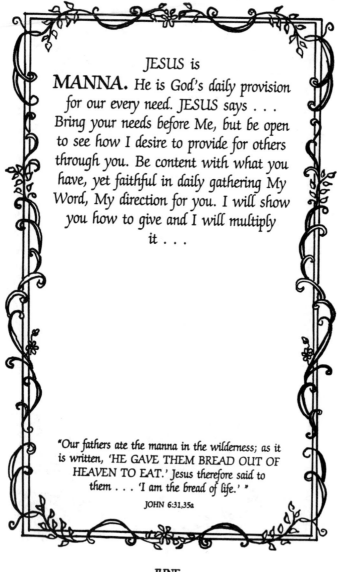

JESUS is

MANNA. He is God's daily provision for our every need. JESUS says . . . Bring your needs before Me, but be open to see how I desire to provide for others through you. Be content with what you have, yet faithful in daily gathering My Word, My direction for you. I will show you how to give and I will multiply it . . .

"Our fathers ate the manna in the wilderness; as it is written, 'HE GAVE THEM BREAD OUT OF HEAVEN TO EAT.' Jesus therefore said to them . . . 'I am the bread of life.' "

JOHN 6:31,35a

JESUS is the
MOST HIGH.

Far above all rulers and authorities, Jesus sits at the right hand of God on the throne of heaven. Since He knows our condition, Jesus understands and is intensely concerned for our welfare. He says . . . No matter what Satan uses to torment you, My authority is far greater. Rely on Me. Learn the power available to you in My name . . .

"Following after Paul and us, she kept crying out, saying, 'These men are bond-servants of the Most High God, who are proclaiming to you the way of salvation' . . . But Paul was greatly annoyed, and turned and said to the spirit, 'I command you in the name of Jesus Christ to come out of her!' And it came out at that very moment."

ACTS 16:17–186

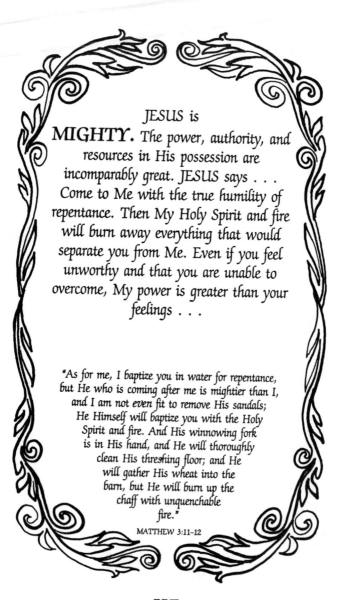

JESUS is
MIGHTY. The power, authority, and resources in His possession are incomparably great. JESUS says . . . Come to Me with the true humility of repentance. Then My Holy Spirit and fire will burn away everything that would separate you from Me. Even if you feel unworthy and that you are unable to overcome, My power is greater than your feelings . . .

"As for me, I baptize you in water for repentance, but He who is coming after me is mightier than I, and I am not even fit to remove His sandals; He Himself will baptize you with the Holy Spirit and fire. And His winnowing fork is in His hand, and He will thoroughly clean His threshing floor; and He will gather His wheat into the barn, but He will burn up the chaff with unquenchable fire."

MATTHEW 3:11–12

JESUS is
MEDIATOR.

He gave His life as a ransom for
mankind, who could not meet the just
demands of a holy God. He says . . .
Even now I am available to stand
between you and the person who has
offended you. Let Me create in you a new
heart, one which forgives, one which
desires reconciliation to the point of giving
up your need to be right . . .

"For there is one God, and one mediator also between
God and men, *the* man Christ Jesus who gave
Himself as a ransom for all, the testimony
borne at the proper time . . . Therefore, I
want men in every place to pray, lifting
up holy hands, without wrath and
dissension."

I TIMOTHY 2:5–6,8

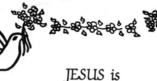

JESUS is
MEEK. He endured injury with
patience and without resentment, being
submissive unto death to God's will for
Him. JESUS says . . . Use all the energy
of your anger to do warfare against the
principalities and powers of darkness. Let
Me train you to be a sharply honed
instrument of intercession. You need not
raise your voice, but in tune with the
Father, speak the word of faith which
causes demonic powers to tremble . . .

"Now I, Paul, myself urge you by the meekness and
gentleness of Christ . . . For though we walk in
the flesh, we do not war according to the flesh,
for the weapons of our warfare are not of the
flesh, but divinely powerful for the
destruction of fortresses. We are
destroying speculations and every
lofty thing raised up against the
knowledge of God, and we are
taking every thought captive
to the obedience of
Christ."

II CORINTHIANS 10:1a,3–5

JUNE
24

JESUS is our
MINISTER. He comes to us as a
host, friend, and teacher with the attitude
of a willing servant. No task is too
menial for Him in His desire to draw us
close to God. JESUS says . . . Are you
bored, angry, despairing of your place in
life? Put off that old nature and look to
Me. Ask Me what I would do, and I will
show you ways to serve in joy . . .

" . . . but whosoever will be great among you, shall
be your minister . . . For even the Son of Man
came not to be ministered unto, but to
minister, and to give his life a ransom for
many."

MARK 10:43b,45 KJV

JESUS is
MERCIFUL.

He is full of mercy; compassionate.
JESUS says . . . I understand what you
are going through. Are you tempted
beyond what you think you can handle?
Give that struggle to Me. Look to Me.
Cling to Me. I am your Savior and
Helper. My compassion is toward you to
heal that aching part. Rest and delight in
Me . . .

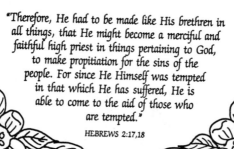

"Therefore, He had to be made like His brethren in
all things, that He might become a merciful and
faithful high priest in things pertaining to God,
to make propitiation for the sins of the
people. For since He Himself was tempted
in that which He has suffered, He is
able to come to the aid of those who
are tempted."

HEBREWS 2:17,18

JESUS is the
MORNING STAR. He is the
bright herald that darkness is past and
that the eternal day where God alone
reigns is dawning. JESUS says . . .
Welcome Me. Welcome Me into your
secret places. Let My light shine on you
so that when I come in fullness of glory
there will be no place in you to make you
ashamed . . .

"And so we have the prophetic word made more sure,
to which you do well to pay attention as to a
lamp shining in a dark place, until the day
dawns and the morning star arises in your
hearts."

II PETER 1:19

JESUS is
MEASURELESS.

There is no observable limit to His greatness, goodness, and power. Without measure He pours His Spirit upon all who will receive. JESUS says . . . As the sun burns constantly and holds your planet in rhythm with the movement of other planets, so My love for you burns constant. Turn to Me with all your mind, emotions, and spirit that I may bathe and fill you to overflowing with My love . . .

"For He whom God has sent speaks the words of God; for He gives the Spirit without measure. The Father loves the Son, and has given all things into His hand."

JOHN 3:34–35

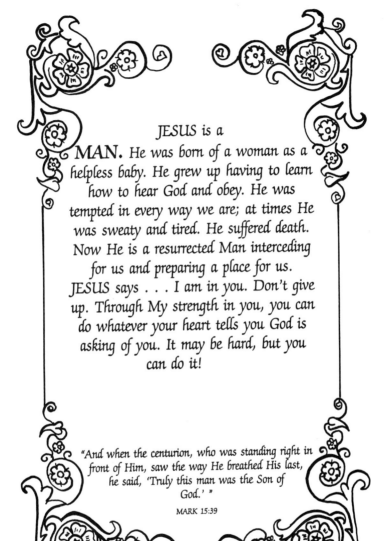

JESUS is a
MAN. He was born of a woman as a
helpless baby. He grew up having to learn
how to hear God and obey. He was
tempted in every way we are; at times He
was sweaty and tired. He suffered death.
Now He is a resurrected Man interceding
for us and preparing a place for us.
JESUS says . . . I am in you. Don't give
up. Through My strength in you, you can
do whatever your heart tells you God is
asking of you. It may be hard, but you
can do it!

"And when the centurion, who was standing right in
front of Him, saw the way He breathed His last,
he said, 'Truly this man was the Son of
God.' "

MARK 15:39

JUNE
29

JESUS is
MESSENGER of the
COVENANT. He is coming again to cleanse, to establish God's Kingdom on earth. JESUS says . . . Now is the time to hate your sin. Now is the time to ask for My Holy Spirit and fire to melt every hardness, remove every bitterness and rebellion from you and from your nation. Now is the time to be ready, for the day of My coming is soon . . .

" 'BEHOLD, I am going to send My messenger, and he will clear the way before Me. And the Lord, whom you seek will suddenly come to His temple; and the messenger of the covenant, in whom you delight, behold, He is coming,' says the LORD of hosts."

MALACHI 3:1

JESUS is
NEW. His broken
body is the New Covenant which has
brought together opposites—Jew and
Gentile, male and female, young and old,
rich and poor, black and white. He
says . . . As you look to Me, I will wash
you free from prejudice. I set you free to
love, to forgive, to demonstrate My
compassion in your circumstances and in
the world . . .

"Since therefore, brethren, we have confidence to enter
the holy place by the blood of Jesus, by a new and
living way which He inaugurated for us
through the veil, that is, His flesh, and since
we have a greater priest over the house of
God, let us draw near with a sincere
heart in full assurance of faith,
having our hearts sprinkled clean
from an evil conscience and
our bodies washed with
pure water."
HEBREWS 10:19–22

JESUS is
NIGH. He is as close
as our breathing. JESUS says . . . Why
do you anxiously search for Me in far
places? I am right here with you. I will
never leave you or forsake you once you
have invited Me into your life. Let Me
touch your broken heart and your contrite
spirit with healing . . .

" . . . The word is nigh thee, even in thy mouth,
and in thy heart: that is, the word of faith, which
we preach: That if thou shalt confess with thy
mouth the Lord Jesus, and shalt believe in
thine heart that God hath raised Him
from the dead, thou shalt be saved."

ROMANS 10:8,9 KJV

JESUS is the
NAZARENE.

God planned to enter history through His
people, the Jews, into a specific place,
Nazareth, by a single mother, Mary. Jesus
was a man in every way. He had a
nationality, a personality, and an address,
the carpenter's shop. JESUS says . . . Do
not be afraid of Me. I know how it feels
to walk in your shoes. Try walking in
Mine . . .

"And being warned by God in a dream, he departed
for the regions of Galilee, and came and resided in
a city called Nazareth, that what was spoken
through the prophets might be fulfilled, 'He
shall be called a Nazarene.' "

MATTHEW 2:22b–23

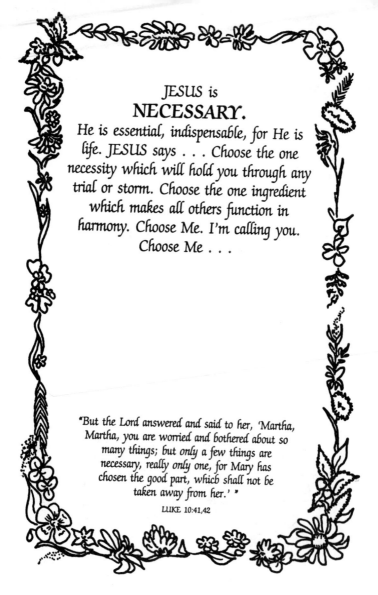

JESUS is
NECESSARY.

He is essential, indispensable, for He is
life. JESUS says . . . Choose the one
necessity which will hold you through any
trial or storm. Choose the one ingredient
which makes all others function in
harmony. Choose Me. I'm calling you.
Choose Me . . .

"But the Lord answered and said to her, 'Martha,
Martha, you are worried and bothered about so
many things; but only a few things are
necessary, really only one, for Mary has
chosen the good part, which shall not be
taken away from her.' "

LUKE 10:41,42

JULY
4

JESUS is the
NAME of SALVATION.
His name delivers us from the power and
effects of sin. JESUS says . . . My name
is more than a word; when you take My
name we become **ONE**. All the benefits
of My cleansing and creative life are yours
as you walk day by day with Me. You
become like the One you love . . .

"And there is salvation in no one else; for there is no
other name under heaven that has been given
among men, by which we must be saved."

ACTS 4:12

JESUS is the
NAME ABOVE
ALL NAMES. He is the very nature and
physical expression of God Himself.
JESUS says . . . When you see Me you
will bow—all the pride in your own
ways will recognize the One greater, the
Source of all accomplishment. Nations
will bow. But I show you My glory now
so that you can enjoy it with Me as
friend, as bride, as co-laborers in the
harvest.

"Therefore also God highly exalted Him, and
bestowed on Him the name which is above every
name, that at the name of Jesus every knee
should bow, of those who are in heaven and
on earth, and under the earth, and that
every tongue should confess that Jesus
Christ is Lord, to the glory of God
the Father."

PHILIPPIANS 2:9–11

JESUS is our
OFFERING.

Since we were unable to give anything
which would please God and fulfill the
agreement, He fulfilled it Himself in
Jesus. He says . . . Your response to My
gift of an open door to relationship with
God is your own life laid down. Seek Me
and I will please God through you. As
you walk in My steps, the desires of your
spirit, which I give you, will be
fulfilled . . .

"THEREFORE be imitators of God, as beloved
children; and walk in love, just as Christ also
loved you, and gave Himself up for us, an
offering and a sacrifice to God as a fragrant
aroma."

EPHESIANS 5:1,2

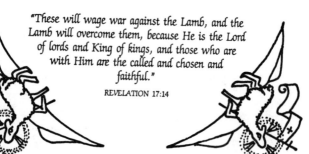

JESUS is the
OVERCOMER.
He has triumphed over all difficulties and
has overwhelmed Satan, the world, and
the physical desires which lead us away
from God. JESUS says . . . Hate the evil
in yourself and in the world, but let the
passion of that hatred operate to bring
forth good. Yearn with Me for all people,
including yourself, to come into the
glorious light of My joy in being
overcomers . . .

"These will wage war against the Lamb, and the
Lamb will overcome them, because He is the Lord
of lords and King of kings, and those who are
with Him are the called and chosen and
faithful."

REVELATION 17:14

JESUS is the
OLIVE TREE.

The olive tree and its fruit in Israel was
used for food, fuel, light, carpentry,
ointments, and medicine. It was a
necessity which grew luxuriantly for
hundreds of years enduring frequent dry
periods. JESUS says . . . On the Mount
of Olives I prayed for you. In the garden
of the olive press I was cut down, but
have come to you again. Bind yourself to
Me and grow . . .

"His shoots will sprout, And his beauty will be like
an olive tree, And his fragrance like the cedars of
Lebanon."

HOSEA 14:6

JESUS is the
OINTMENT.

In ancient times ointment was used for cleansing, as perfume, in hospitality, as a sign of joy, for medicine, in the mortuary process, on shields, and in consecration. JESUS says . . . Receive the anointing I have for you. It heals your inner hurts, your body, and cleanses you from past wrongs. Receive with joy your place in My Kingdom . . .

"Your oils have a pleasing fragrance, Your name is like purified oil."

SONG OF SOLOMON 1:3

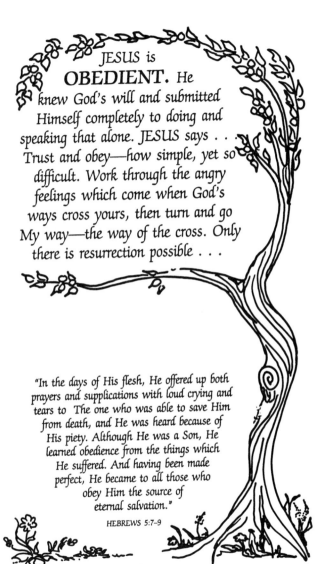

JESUS is **OBEDIENT.** He knew God's will and submitted Himself completely to doing and speaking that alone. JESUS says . . . Trust and obey—how simple, yet so difficult. Work through the angry feelings which come when God's ways cross yours, then turn and go My way—the way of the cross. Only there is resurrection possible . . .

"In the days of His flesh, He offered up both prayers and supplications with loud crying and tears to The one who was able to save Him from death, and He was heard because of His piety. Although He was a Son, He learned obedience from the things which He suffered. And having been made perfect, He became to all those who obey Him the source of eternal salvation."

HEBREWS 5:7–9

JULY
11

JESUS is the **OMEGA.** As everything began in Him, so will everything end in Him. This is our confidence. JESUS says . . . As you see the systems of the world crumble about you, as you see antichrists reign, as you see the earth's resources stripped and misused, rejoice, for the end is near. Pray that in their distress all who would love Me will come and enter into My new beginning. Be part of that solution . . .

"And He said to me, 'It is done. I am the Alpha and the Omega, the beginning and the end. I will give to the one who thirsts from the spring of the water of life without cost. He who overcomes shall inherit these things, and I will be his God and he will be My son.' "

REVELATION 21:6,7

JESUS is the
ONLY BEGOTTEN SON.
He is unique; there is no one
else like Him. JESUS
says . . . Through Me
many can become sons of God,
all who believe and receive Me.
Pray that the glory of My
Presence shines through you to draw
others into My family . . .

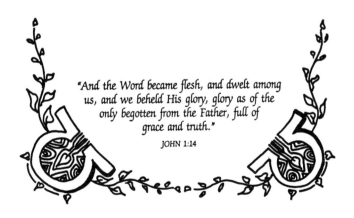

"And the Word became flesh, and dwelt among
us, and we beheld His glory, glory as of the
only begotten from the Father, full of
grace and truth."

JOHN 1:14

JESUS is our
PROPHET. He is the one who
understands history because He knows
intimately and demonstrates God's
concerns, purposes, and actions. He
says . . . Today where there is unbelief, I
am able to do little. Get in the place that
feeds your belief in Me. Find those who
are joyous in Me, who know that greater
things are happening now than when I
walked in Galilee . . .

"And the multitudes were saying, 'This is the
prophet, Jesus, from Nazareth in Galilee.' And
Jesus entered the temple and cast out all those
who were buying and selling in the temple
. . . And the blind and the lame came to
Him in the temple, and He healed
them."

MATTHEW 21:11–12a,14

JESUS is our
PRIEST. He is the
sinless mediator between God and man.
His death tore the veil to the Holy of
Holies so that through Him believers can
minister to God and hear what is on His
heart. JESUS says . . . Royal priesthood,
holy nation, I have called you to be this.
I have chosen you. Learn of Me how to
minister to the Lord and to your brothers.
There is nothing greater . . .

"But when Christ appeared as a high priest of the
good things to come, He entered through the
greater and more perfect tabernacle, not made
with hands . . . but through His own blood,
He entered the holy place once for all,
having obtained eternal redemption."

HEBREWS 9:11a–12b

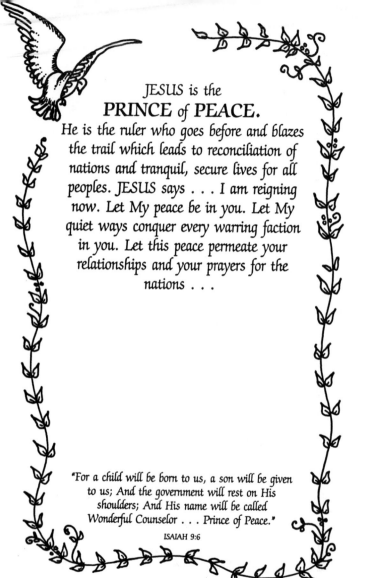

JESUS is the
PRINCE of PEACE.

He is the ruler who goes before and blazes
the trail which leads to reconciliation of
nations and tranquil, secure lives for all
peoples. JESUS says . . . I am reigning
now. Let My peace be in you. Let My
quiet ways conquer every warring faction
in you. Let this peace permeate your
relationships and your prayers for the
nations . . .

"For a child will be born to us, a son will be given
to us; And the government will rest on His
shoulders; And His name will be called
Wonderful Counselor . . . Prince of Peace."

ISAIAH 9:6

JULY
16

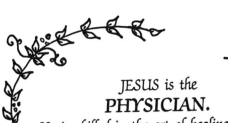

JESUS is the
PHYSICIAN.

He is skilled in the art of healing. JESUS
says, Come to Me with all your wounds,
your hurts, resentments, disappointments,
and bitterness. With love I will cut away
the malignant growth, tenderly knit
together your relationships, and make you
whole . . .

"Why do you eat and drink with the tax-gatherers
and sinners?" And Jesus answered and said to
them, "It *is* not those who are well who need
a physician, but those who are sick. I have
not come to call righteous men but
sinners to repentance."

LUKE 5:30b–32

JESUS is the
PRINCE of LIFE.

Abundant life, health and joy in the midst of persecutions Jesus offers to those who choose Him as LORD. He says . . . Greater things than I have done shall you do, I told the disciples. I promise the same to My followers today. It will cost you everything to follow Me, but the victory over sin, sickness, and grief will flow through you to touch many. Come quickly; time is short. . .

"[You] . . . put to death the Prince of life, the one whom God raised from the dead, a fact to which we are witnesses. And on the basis of faith in His name, it is the name of Jesus which has strengthened this man whom you see and know; and the faith which comes through Him has given him this perfect health in the presence of you all."

ACTS 3:15–16

JESUS is our
PARACLETE.

He always intercedes for us and stands close by to help us. He sends another Paraclete, the Holy Spirit, to be our Counselor and to enable us to witness with power. JESUS says . . . After Pentecost the disciples asked for boldness to witness. To answer that prayer, I filled them again with My Holy Spirit. You cannot have too much Holy Spirit. Just ask . . .

"My little children, I am writing these things to you that you may not sin. And if anyone sins, we have an Advocate* [PARACLETE] with the Father, Jesus Christ the righteous."
*Transliteration from the Greek.

I JOHN 2:1

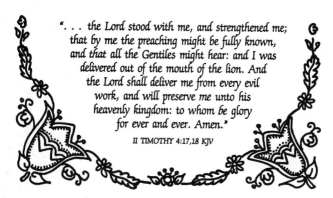

JESUS is our
PRESERVER.
He keeps us safe, delivers, protects, heals
and makes us whole. JESUS says . . .
All the protections the world offers will go
down. Paul trusted Me in everything and
he had shipwrecks, beatings,
imprisonment. He had suffering with joy
and is with Me reigning eternally. Which
life saver do you choose?

". . . the Lord stood with me, and strengthened me;
that by me the preaching might be fully known,
and that all the Gentiles might hear: and I was
delivered out of the mouth of the lion. And
the Lord shall deliver me from every evil
work, and will preserve me unto his
heavenly kingdom: to whom be glory
for ever and ever. Amen."

II TIMOTHY 4:17,18 KJV

JESUS is
PATIENT. He bears
up under pain or evil with endurance and
is gentle toward those who hurt Him.
JESUS says . . . When you cannot say,
'Father, forgive them,' call upon Me to
love through you. When you feel you
cannot go another step, reach out to Me,
and I will carry you through . . .

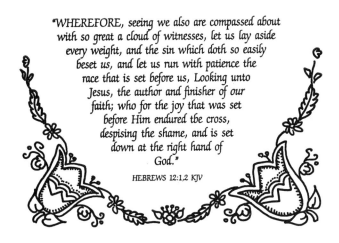

"WHEREFORE, seeing we also are compassed about
with so great a cloud of witnesses, let us lay aside
every weight, and the sin which doth so easily
beset us, and let us run with patience the
race that is set before us, Looking unto
Jesus, the author and finisher of our
faith; who for the joy that was set
before Him endured the cross,
despising the shame, and is set
down at the right hand of
God."

HEBREWS 12:1,2 KJV

JESUS is the
PRINCE of KINGS.
He is the ruler over all other authorities
and powers of earth. JESUS says . . .
Take the authority I give you to cast
down the rulers of darkness who exalt
themselves in your land. Bind them with
the unbreakable ropes of My blood. Pray
for your leaders to submit to My rule and
give allegiance to GOD . . .

" . . . Jesus Christ, *who is the faithful witness, and
the first begotten of the dead, and the prince of the
kings of the earth. Unto him that loved us, and
washed us from our sins in his own blood.
And hath made us kings and priests unto
God and his Father; to him be glory
and dominion for ever and ever.
Amen.*"

REVELATION 1:5,6 KJV

JESUS is our

PASSOVER.

He is our celebration and remembrance
that God has spared us from the angel of
death by the sacrifice of the perfect Lamb.
JESUS says . . . My blood covers the
doorway of your heart. Rejoice and
tremble with thanksgiving. Pray for My
people who celebrate Passover without
discerning My Body . . .

"Clean out the old leaven, that you may be a new
lump, just as you are in fact unleavened. For
Christ our Passover also has been sacrificed. Let
us therefore celebrate the feast, not with old
leaven, nor with the leaven of malice and
wickedness, but with the unleavened
bread of sincerity and truth."

I CORINTHIANS 5:7,8

JESUS is our **PEACE.** He is our security and tranquility both within ourselves, in our relationships, and among the nations. He is the SHALOM of Jew and Christian. JESUS says . . . The world wants a peace of selfishness— where everyone could get his own way. My peace means putting down your ways which keep others from seeing Me. My peace is the hard work of tearing down false walls of fear and prejudice, so that love can build . . .

"For He Himself is our peace, who made both groups into one, and broke down the barrier of the dividing wall, by abolishing in His flesh the enmity, which is the Law of commandments contained in ordinances, that in Himself He might make the two into one new man, thus establishing peace, and might reconcile them both in one body to God through the cross."

EPHESIANS 2:14–16a

JESUS is the
POTENTATE.
He is the one who wields controlling
power. JESUS says . . . Flee from the
longing for money, which is the root of all
evil. Pursue righteousness, godliness,
faith, love, perseverance, and gentleness.
Fight the good fight of faith; take hold of
the eternal life to which you were called
. . . Hold fast, for My power will enable
you to do what I ask . . .

". . . keep this commandment without spot,
unrebukable, until the appearing of our Lord Jesus
Christ: Which in his times he shall shew, who
is the blessed and only Potentate, the King
of kings, and Lord of lords."

I TIMOTHY 6:14,15 KJV

JESUS is the
PLEASURE of GOD.
His obedience and responsiveness are the
sources of God's delight and joy. JESUS
says . . . My Father's pleasure and mine
are one, though there was terrible agony
for Me in opening the way for you to
know God as I know Him. How He joys
in knowing you love Him and give your
life to please Him. In that is your true
happiness . . .

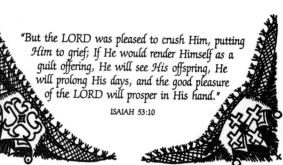

"But the LORD was pleased to crush Him, putting
Him to grief; If He would render Himself as a
guilt offering, He will see His offspring, He
will prolong His days, and the good pleasure
of the LORD will prosper in His hand."

ISAIAH 53:10

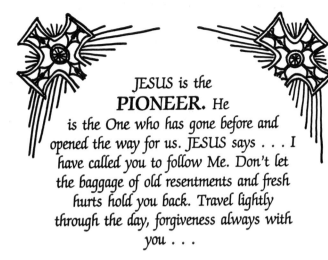

JESUS is the
PIONEER. He
is the One who has gone before and
opened the way for us. JESUS says . . . I
have called you to follow Me. Don't let
the baggage of old resentments and fresh
hurts hold you back. Travel lightly
through the day, forgiveness always with
you . . .

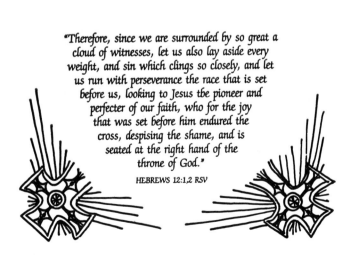

"Therefore, since we are surrounded by so great a
cloud of witnesses, let us also lay aside every
weight, and sin which clings so closely, and let
us run with perseverance the race that is set
before us, looking to Jesus the pioneer and
perfecter of our faith, who for the joy
that was set before him endured the
cross, despising the shame, and is
seated at the right hand of the
throne of God."

HEBREWS 12:1,2 RSV

JESUS is the
POWER of GOD.
He is the miraculous force which is
abundant and mighty in ability to get the
job done. JESUS says . . . My power is
in you. Believe this. The power in you is
greater than the powers of the world. Let
Me use you to overcome strongholds of
Satan in prayer, to release the captives,
and to proclaim Jubilee . . .

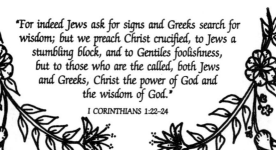

"For indeed Jews ask for signs and Greeks search for
wisdom; but we preach Christ crucified, to Jews a
stumbling block, and to Gentiles foolishness,
but to those who are the called, both Jews
and Greeks, Christ the power of God and
the wisdom of God."

I CORINTHIANS 1:22–24

JESUS is the **PRIZE.** He is the imperishable wreath, the award at the end of the race. In Him all our preparations, discipline, and effort in running the race work together with God's promises for our good. JESUS says . . . Let My Word and My Spirit train you and coach you in the things of God. You can do much more than you ever dreamed . . . and you have My love to give . . .

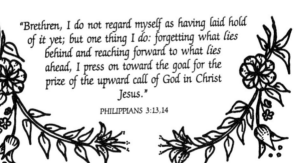

"Brethren, I do not regard myself as having laid hold of it yet; but one thing I do: forgetting what lies behind and reaching forward to what lies ahead, I press on toward the goal for the prize of the upward call of God in Christ Jesus."

PHILIPPIANS 3:13,14

JESUS is the
LION of JUDAH.
He is the mighty, unconquerable King from David's line, the promised King of Israel. JESUS says . . . How I long for My people to see in the shamed, slain One the very answer to their desires for a triumphant king. That day will come when all will see. Prepare for that day by knowing Me and sharing Me.

". . . and one of the elders said to me, 'Stop weeping; behold the Lion that is from the tribe of Judah, the Root of David, has overcome so as to open the book and its seven seals.' "

REVELATION 5:5

JESUS is the
PURIFIER.

All who ask for His baptism of fire
become clean and bright. He makes us
pure and innocent as young children.
JESUS says . . . Bring to Me all that
you are. Ask for My fire so that all, not
of Me, will burn, be cleansed away, now.
Burn the straw to make room for My
pure gold and precious stones in your
building . . .

"And He will sit as a smelter and purifier of silver,
and He will purify the sons of Levi and refine
them like gold and silver, so that they may
present to the LORD offerings in
righteousness."

MALACHI 3:3

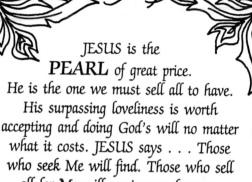

JESUS is the
PEARL of great price.
He is the one we must sell all to have.
His surpassing loveliness is worth
accepting and doing God's will no matter
what it costs. JESUS says . . . Those
who seek Me will find. Those who sell
all for Me will receive much more.
Luminous, glowing, iridescent, I bring
peace and beauty to all who are
mine . . .

"Again, the kingdom of heaven is like a merchant
seeking fine pearls, and upon finding one pearl of
great value, he went and sold all that he had,
and bought it."

MATTHEW 13:45,46

JESUS is the
PIERCED.

Nails were hammered into His hands and
feet. A sword was thrust through His
side; blood and water, His life, poured
onto the ground for us. JESUS says . . .
Look on Me and know that My love for
you is eternal. Look on Me, the pierced,
and long for My own chosen, the Jews,
to see what you see. Soften the hard
ground with weeping for My people . . . .

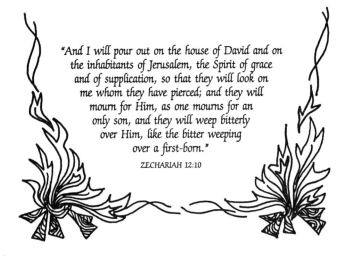

"And I will pour out on the house of David and on
the inhabitants of Jerusalem, the Spirit of grace
and of supplication, so that they will look on
me whom they have pierced; and they will
mourn for Him, as one mourns for an
only son, and they will weep bitterly
over Him, like the bitter weeping
over a first-born."

ZECHARIAH 12:10

JESUS is
PRAISEWORTHY.

Around the throne the angels and thousands upon thousands of faithful declare that Jesus is worthy to receive power, and riches, and wisdom, and might, and glory, and honor, and blessing. JESUS says . . . As you enter into high praise with those who have gone through death, you will find new release from cares of the world, new purpose, new perspective, new power to witness, and new joy . . .

"And the peace of God, which surpasses all comprehension, shall guard your hearts and your minds in Christ Jesus. Finally, brethren, whatever is true, whatever is honorable, whatever is right, whatever is pure, whatever is lovely, whatever is of good repute, if there is any excellence, and if anything worthy of praise, let your mind dwell on these things."

PHILIPPIANS 4:7,8

JESUS is
PRECIOUS.

He is of the greatest value. JESUS says . . . Why spend your money for things which tear up and are obsolete in a year? Why value the things of the world which are destroyed by dust, moths, or rust? Build your life and relationships with the gentle things money can't buy and build on Me. When you see My heart crying out for lost ones all over the world and in your own neighborhood and town, your heart will begin to weep, too, and My building is begun . . .

"Therefore thus saith the Lord God, Behold I lay in Zion for a foundation a stone, a tried stone, a precious corner *stone*, a sure foundation" (KJV). "He who believes *in it* will not be disturbed"(NAS).

ISAIAH 28:16

JESUS is
PERCEPTIVE.
He is discerning of the thoughts and
motives of our hearts. He knows us
thoroughly. JESUS says, Though you may
fool yourself, I know you well and I love
you. Allow My truth to penetrate you and
My love to forgive and heal you.
I can do it . . .

"But when Jesus perceived their thoughts, he
answering said unto them, What reason ye in
your hearts? Whether is easier, to say, Thy sins
be forgiven thee; or to say, Rise up and
walk? But that ye may know that the
Son of Man hath power upon earth to
forgive sins, he said unto the sick of
the palsy, I say unto thee, Arise."

LUKE 5:22-24 KJV

JESUS is
PERFECT.

He is complete in every way. He has
satisfied all God's requirements and is
entirely without fault or defect. JESUS
says . . . I will complete you by teaching
you My ways and bring you, with all
others who will come, into that perfectly
functioning body where I am
the Head . . .

"And he gave some, apostles; and some, prophets;
and some, evangelists; and some pastors and
teachers; For the perfecting of the saints, For
the work of the ministry, for the edifying of
the body of Christ: Till we all come in
the unity of the faith, and of the
knowledge of the Son of God, unto
a perfect man, unto the measure
of the stature of the fullness of
Christ."

EPHESIANS 4:11–13 KJV

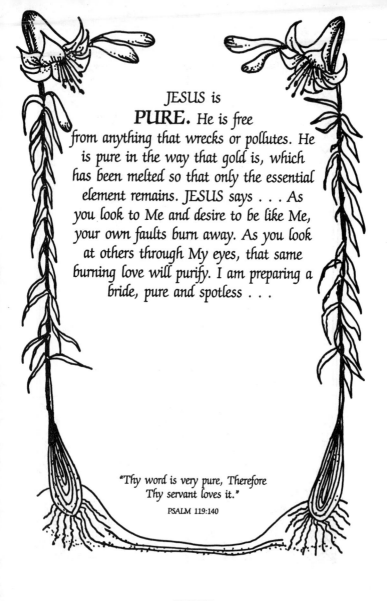

JESUS is
PURE. He is free
from anything that wrecks or pollutes. He
is pure in the way that gold is, which
has been melted so that only the essential
element remains. JESUS says . . . As
you look to Me and desire to be like Me,
your own faults burn away. As you look
at others through My eyes, that same
burning love will purify. I am preparing a
bride, pure and spotless . . .

"Thy word is very pure, Therefore
Thy servant loves it."

PSALM 119:140

JESUS is
PERSECUTED.

In His earthly life He was harassed,
grieved, tortured, and put to violent death.
Today, in many parts of the world, Jesus
is still persecuted in His Body on earth.
JESUS says . . . Father, forgive them.
They don't know what they are doing!
Love those who have not experienced My
love as you have. Pray for them to see in
you, as Saul saw in Stephen, a light and
reality which persecution and even death
cannot stamp out . . .

"Remember the word that I said to you. 'A slave is
not greater than his master.' If they persecuted
Me, they will also persecute you; if they kept
My word, they will keep yours also. But all
these things they will do to you for My
name's sake, because they do not know
the One who sent Me."

JOHN 15:20,21

JESUS is the
QUICKENING SPIRIT.
He gives us vibrant, abundant life and after death, a body like His own imperishable one. JESUS says . . . Why settle for business as usual? Why struggle to survive? In Me your life becomes filled with challenges which I accomplish through you. In Me your life is a training ground for the adventures of the life to come. Enjoy My life now . . . ·

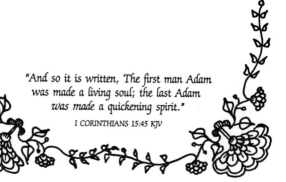

"And so it is written, The first man Adam was made a living soul; the last Adam was made a quickening spirit."

I CORINTHIANS 15:45 KJV

JESUS is the
QUICKENER. He
vitalizes, makes us alive, gives us full and
abundant life. JESUS says . . . As you
enter into My gates with thanksgiving
and into My courts with praise, your
spirit, mind, and body are filled with the
very source of life. Be filled with My
Spirit of joy and holiness and of tender
weeping for those who have not come to
Me. Your tears soften their hearts and
enable them to come to Me.

"For as the Father raiseth up the dead, and
quickeneth *them;* even so the Son quickeneth
whom he will. For the Father judgeth no man,
but hath committed all judgment unto the
Son; That all *men* should honour the
Son, even as they honour the Father."

JOHN 5:21–23a KJV

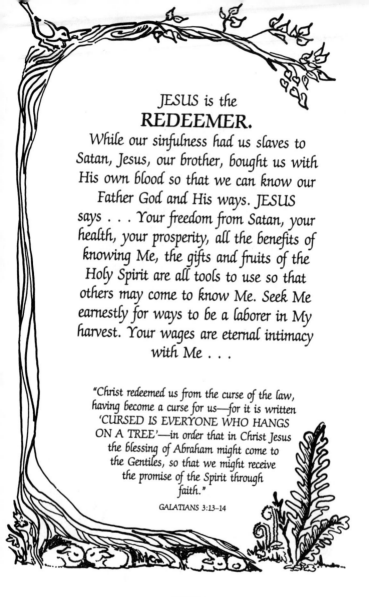

JESUS is the
REDEEMER.

While our sinfulness had us slaves to Satan, Jesus, our brother, bought us with His own blood so that we can know our Father God and His ways. JESUS says . . . Your freedom from Satan, your health, your prosperity, all the benefits of knowing Me, the gifts and fruits of the Holy Spirit are all tools to use so that others may come to know Me. Seek Me earnestly for ways to be a laborer in My harvest. Your wages are eternal intimacy with Me . . .

"Christ redeemed us from the curse of the law, having become a curse for us—for it is written 'CURSED IS EVERYONE WHO HANGS ON A TREE'—in order that in Christ Jesus the blessing of Abraham might come to the Gentiles, so that we might receive the promise of the Spirit through faith."

GALATIANS 3:13–14

JESUS is the
REPAIRER. He strengthens and
rebuilds the ancient foundation walls
which resist the evil powers of the world.
JESUS says . . . Some walls must be
broken down—walls of pride and
prejudice. Others must be restored.
Examine your heart to see what has
broken in you that God approves. These
walls I rebuild in you and in My Body.
The plumbline is My Word. Build with
Me . . .

"And those from among you will rebuild the ancient
ruins; You will raise up the age-old foundations;
And you will be called the repairer of the
breach, The restorer of the streets in which
to dwell."

ISAIAH 58:12

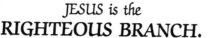

JESUS is the
RIGHTEOUS BRANCH.

He is the just one, the Jew who
completely fufilled the law God gave to
Israel. JESUS says . . . Immerse yourself
in Me and in My Word so that you know
what pleases God. I know the motives
and desires of your heart. I wash you and
enable you to do what is right . . .

"Behold, the days are coming," declares the Lord,
"when I shall raise up for David a righteous
Branch; And He will do justice and
righteousness in the land. In His days Judah
will be saved. And Israel will dwell
securely; And this is His name by
which He will be called, 'The
LORD our righteousness.'"

JEREMIAH 23:5,6

JESUS is the
REFINER. His baptism with fire
melts us to remove all impurities from us
so that our bodies as living sacrifices will
be holy, acceptable, pleasing to God.
JESUS says . . . Doesn't your heart burn
within you when you hear Me speak to
you? Don't I apply the purifying fires of
circumstances and relationships with
gentleness? I melt you within and without
until all that remains is praise . . .

"And who can stand when He appears. For He is
like a refiner's fire and like fuller's soap. And He
will sit as a smelter and purifier of silver, and
He will purify the sons of Levi and refine
them like gold and silver, so that they
may present to the Lord offerings in
righteousness."

MALACHI 3:2b–3

JESUS is our
REFUGE. He is our
shelter, our hope. We can trust Him to be
our protection from danger or distress.
JESUS says . . . Come to Me for the
burning away of everything which is not
of God. Come to Me for protection from
the angry, fiery darts of the evil one. My
Presence and My glory are your covering
and your delight . . .

"When the Lord has washed away the filth of the
daughters of Zion, and purged the bloodshed of
Jerusalem from her midst, by the spirit of judgment
and the spirit of burning, then the LORD will
create over the whole area of Mount Zion and
over her assemblies a cloud by day, even smoke,
and the brightness of a flaming fire by night;
for over all the glory will be a canopy. And
there will be a shelter to give shade from
the heat by day, and refuge and protection
from the storm and the rain."

ISAIAH 4:4–6

JESUS is our

RULER. As a shepherd is gentle
toward his sheep, yet strong and vigorous
against the enemies of his flock, so is
Jesus as our Ruler. He says . . . All My
authority is tempered with mercy. Do the
same if you measure your life by My rule.
Let My ways of peace rule in your
emotions and thoughts. My ways yield
the sweet fruit of self-control . . .

"For as in Adam all die, so also in Christ all shall be
made alive. But each in his own order: Christ the
first fruits, after that those who are Christ's at
His coming, then comes the end, when He
delivers up the kingdom to the God and
Father, when He has abolished all rule
and all authority and power. For He
must reign until He has put all
His enemies under His feet."

I CORINTHIANS 15:22–25

JESUS is our
RIGHTEOUSNESS. He is the
one who presents us before the Father-
Judge, free from guilt and sin. He enables
us to take on His nature which acts in
accord with God's wisdom and moral
law. JESUS says . . . No man is
righteous without Me, but many are
doing right in their own eyes. Cover
yourself with the robes of My Presence.
See, hear, smell, taste, touch, think about
the world and even yourself through the
light of My wisdom and goodness . . .

"Behold, the days are coming," declares the LORD,
"When I shall raise up for David a righteous
Branch; And He will reign as king and act
wisely And do justice and righteousness in
the land. In His days Judah will be saved,
And Israel will dwell securely; And
this is His name by which He will
be called, 'The Lord our
righteousness.'"

JEREMIAH 23:5,6

JESUS is the
RESURRECTION.

In Him the dead are raised and given new life. JESUS says . . . The whole of life is meant to be a glorious expression of praise and enjoyment of God with all who call Him Father. How I weep for those covered with cares of the world or choked by lust for material things and pleasures. Through the tears, call them with Me to 'Come forth' . . .

"Jesus said to her, 'I am the resurrection and the life; he who believes in Me shall live even if he dies, and everyone who lives and believes in Me shall never die. Do you believe this?' "

JOHN 11:25,26

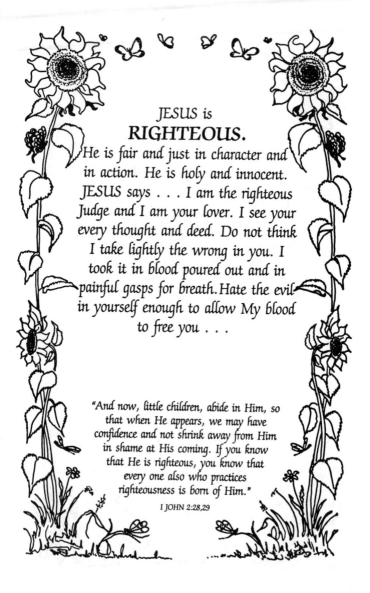

JESUS is
RIGHTEOUS.

He is fair and just in character and in action. He is holy and innocent. JESUS says . . . I am the righteous Judge and I am your lover. I see your every thought and deed. Do not think I take lightly the wrong in you. I took it in blood poured out and in painful gasps for breath. Hate the evil in yourself enough to allow My blood to free you . . .

"And now, little children, abide in Him, so that when He appears, we may have confidence and not shrink away from Him in shame at His coming. If you know that He is righteous, you know that every one also who practices righteousness is born of Him."

I JOHN 2:28,29

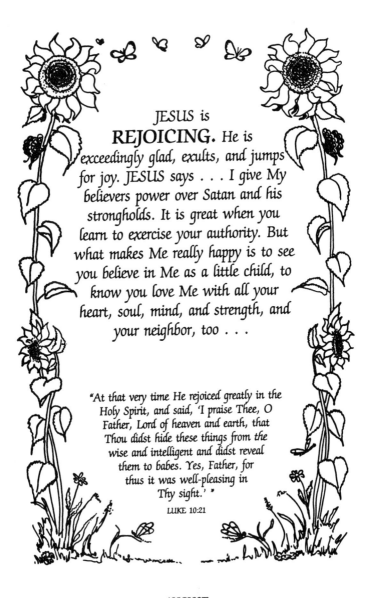

JESUS is **REJOICING.** He is exceedingly glad, exults, and jumps for joy. JESUS says . . . I give My believers power over Satan and his strongholds. It is great when you learn to exercise your authority. But what makes Me really happy is to see you believe in Me as a little child, to know you love Me with all your heart, soul, mind, and strength, and your neighbor, too . . .

"At that very time He rejoiced greatly in the Holy Spirit, and said, 'I praise Thee, O Father, Lord of heaven and earth, that Thou didst hide these things from the wise and intelligent and didst reveal them to babes. Yes, Father, for thus it was well-pleasing in Thy sight.' "

LUKE 10:21

JESUS is
REJECTED.

He was and still is today despised,
rebuffed, refused, repulsed, thrown out as
worthless. JESUS says . . . Many who
have heard My call refuse to come follow
Me. Many who have heard My Word
ridicule it and consider their ways better
than My way. Today I call you to join
Me, even though they will despise and
reject you. Count the cost—it is all or
nothing . . .

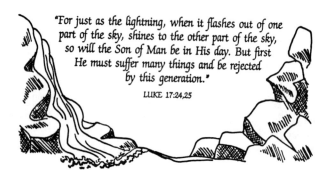

"For just as the lightning, when it flashes out of one
part of the sky, shines to the other part of the sky,
so will the Son of Man be in His day. But first
He must suffer many things and be rejected
by this generation."

LUKE 17:24,25

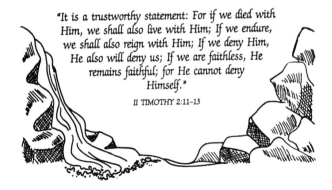

JESUS
REIGNS. He possesses
and exercises sovereign power over all the
governments of earth and over all creation,
visible and invisible. JESUS says . . .
Allow Me to rule in your life. When you
take the reins without consulting Me, the
result is chaos. I balance and order all
things. Be still and know that I am God
so you can with joy fit into and cooperate
with what I am doing . . .

"It is a trustworthy statement: For if we died with
Him, we shall also live with Him; If we endure,
we shall also reign with Him; If we deny Him,
He also will deny us; If we are faithless, He
remains faithful; for He cannot deny
Himself."

II TIMOTHY 2:11–13

JESUS is the
READER of the
BOOK of LIFE. He is worthy to open
the door that was closed to Eden because
He was pure and obedient through death.
He rejoices that our belief in Him records
our names in the Book of Life. JESUS
says . . . I know your heart. It is open to
Me. I know what is written there. Let
My Word cleanse you now of all filth so
that My Name and yours can be indelibly
etched in eternal life . . .

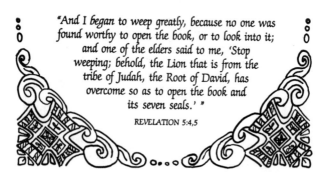

"And I began to weep greatly, because no one was
found worthy to open the book, or to look into it;
and one of the elders said to me, 'Stop
weeping; behold, the Lion that is from the
tribe of Judah, the Root of David, has
overcome so as to open the book and
its seven seals.' "

REVELATION 5:4,5

JESUS is our

RANSOM. His life
and death on the cross are the price paid
for our release from Satan's power over
us, from sin, sickness, death. The debt
we owed to Satan has been paid in full.
JESUS says . . . Accept your deliverance.
Receive My forgiveness. Enter into a new
relationship with Me which expresses the
enjoyment of a slave who has become
free. Your happiness will spill over into
eager giving of yourself to those I show
you, and in prayer for all . . .

"But it is not so among you, but whoever wishes to
become great among you shall be your servant;
and whoever wishes to be first among you shall
be slave of all. For even the Son of Man did
not come to be served, but to serve, and
to give His life a ransom for many."

MARK 10:43–45

JESUS is our
RECONCILIATION.
The estrangement between God and man,
brought about by man's sin, is ended by
Jesus' sacrificial death on the cross.
Gentiles, as well as Jews, find their true
life and spiritual home where Jesus is
Lord. JESUS says . . . When I broke
down the walls separating you from other
kinds of people, I enabled you to see Me
in all who love Me. Take off the blinders
put up by your country, race, even by
your denomination, and appreciate Me in
people everywhere . . .

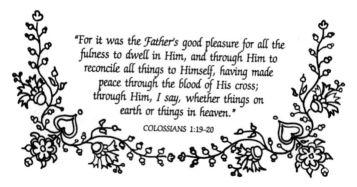

"For it was the Father's good pleasure for all the
fulness to dwell in Him, and through Him to
reconcile all things to Himself, having made
peace through the blood of His cross;
through Him, I say, whether things on
earth or things in heaven."

COLOSSIANS 1:19–20

JESUS is our
REFRESHER. He
enables us to recover our breath and be
revived. In Him our strength is restored.
JESUS says . . . Come to Me, in the
steamy heat of your desires and passions,
for the cooling waters of My Presence.
Apply the ointment of My Holy Spirit on
the burns made by fiery darts of the evil
one. Receive My showers of blessing and
encouragement today . . .

"Repent therefore and return, that your sins may be
wiped away, in order that times of refreshing may
come from the presence of the Lord; and that
He may send Jesus, the Christ appointed for
you, whom heaven must receive until the
period of restoration of all things about
which God spoke by the mouth of
His holy prophets from ancient
time."

ACTS 3:19–21

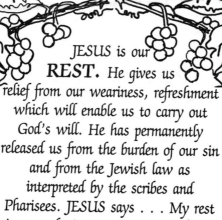

JESUS is our **REST.** He gives us relief from our weariness, refreshment which will enable us to carry out God's will. He has permanently released us from the burden of our sin and from the Jewish law as interpreted by the scribes and Pharisees. JESUS says . . . My rest is never boring, yet it is never busy. My rest is the relationship which John knew as he laid his head on my chest: there he heard My voice, and received strength and love to do My will . . .

"Come to Me, all who are weary and heavyladen, and I will give you rest. Take My yoke upon you, and learn from Me, for I am gentle and humble in heart; and YOU SHALL FIND REST FOR YOUR SOULS. For My yoke is easy, and My load is light."

MATTHEW 11:28–30

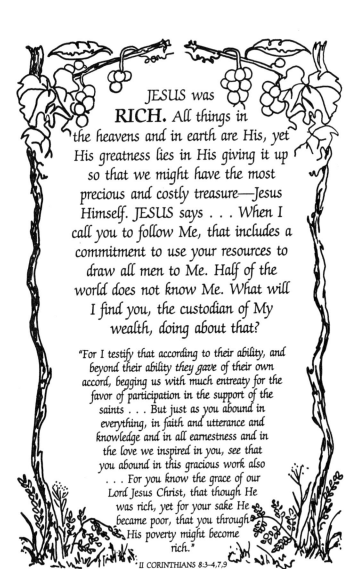

JESUS was **RICH.** All things in the heavens and in earth are His, yet His greatness lies in His giving it up so that we might have the most precious and costly treasure—Jesus Himself. JESUS says . . . When I call you to follow Me, that includes a commitment to use your resources to draw all men to Me. Half of the world does not know Me. What will I find you, the custodian of My wealth, doing about that?

"For I testify that according to their ability, and beyond their ability *they gave* of their own accord, begging us with much entreaty for the favor of participation in the support of the saints . . . But just as you abound in everything, in faith and utterance and knowledge and in all earnestness and in the love we inspired in you, *see that you abound in this gracious work also* . . . For you know the grace of our Lord Jesus Christ, that though He was rich, yet for your sake He became poor, that you through His poverty might become rich."

II CORINTHIANS 8:3–4,7,9

AUGUST
28

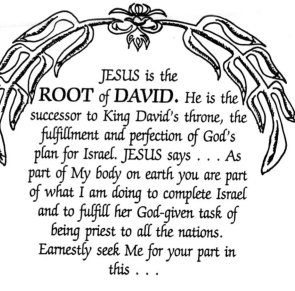

JESUS is the
ROOT of **DAVID**. He is the
successor to King David's throne, the
fulfillment and perfection of God's
plan for Israel. JESUS says . . . As
part of My body on earth you are part
of what I am doing to complete Israel
and to fulfill her God-given task of
being priest to all the nations.
Earnestly seek Me for your part in
this . . .

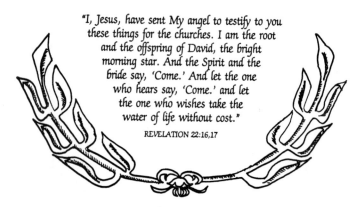

"I, Jesus, have sent My angel to testify to you
these things for the churches. I am the root
and the offspring of David, the bright
morning star. And the Spirit and the
bride say, 'Come.' And let the one
who hears say, 'Come.' and let
the one who wishes take the
water of life without cost."

REVELATION 22:16,17

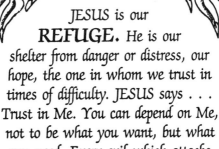

JESUS is our **REFUGE.** He is our shelter from danger or distress, our hope, the one in whom we trust in times of difficulty. JESUS says . . . Trust in Me. You can depend on Me, not to be what you want, but what you need. Every evil which attacks your thoughts, health, finances, loved ones, nation, world, cringes where I am LORD. I lead you through places where evil is powerful. You will enjoy supper with Me even in the presence of your enemies . . .

"When my anxious thoughts multiply within me. Thy consolations delight my soul . . . the LORD has been my stronghold, And my God the rock of my refuge. And He has brought back their wickedness upon them, And will destroy them in their evil; The LORD our God will destroy them."

PSALM 94:19,22–23

JESUS is the
ROCK of OFFENSE.

Because Jesus is God and many had built very different concepts of God, He was rejected. This rejection of Jesus is denial of the true, living God; it causes unbelievers to stumble or sin. JESUS says . . . Look carefully to My WORD. See how I fulfill all the Law and the prophets, though I do not fulfill many of the expectations of Pharisees then or now. Look carefully to Me and build on Me. I am the only sure foundation . . .

"And coming to Him as to a living stone, rejected by men, but choice and precious in the sight of God, you also, as living stones, are being built up as a spiritual house for a holy priesthood, to offer up spiritual sacrifices acceptable to God through Jesus Christ . . . 'THE STONE WHICH THE BUILDERS REJECTED, THIS BECAME THE VERY CORNERSTONE,' AND 'A STONE OF STUMBLING AND A ROCK OF OFFENSE.'"

I PETER 2:4–8

JESUS is our
REDEMPTION.

He is our deliverance from sin and its effects. His blood paid in full the ransom price and set all hostages to Satan free. JESUS says . . . As you forgive others you participate with Me in the loosing of chains which bind you. Freely you have received; freely give . . .

"In Him we have redemption through His blood, the forgiveness of our trespasses, according to the riches of His grace, which He lavished upon us."

EPHESIANS 1:7,8a

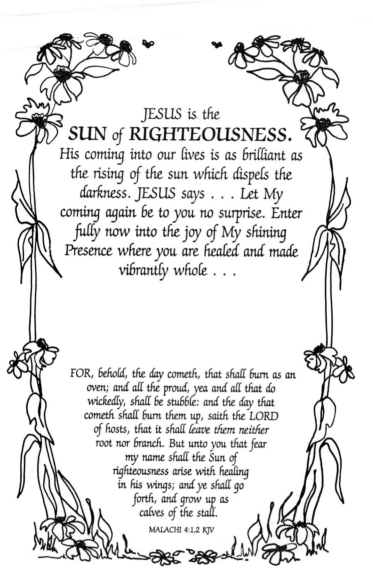

JESUS is the
SUN of RIGHTEOUSNESS.
His coming into our lives is as brilliant as
the rising of the sun which dispels the
darkness. JESUS says . . . Let My
coming again be to you no surprise. Enter
fully now into the joy of My shining
Presence where you are healed and made
vibrantly whole . . .

FOR, behold, the day cometh, that shall burn as an
oven; and all the proud, yea and all that do
wickedly, shall be stubble: and the day that
cometh shall burn them up, saith the LORD
of hosts, that it shall *leave them neither*
root nor branch. But unto you that fear
my name shall the Sun of
righteousness arise with healing
in his wings; and ye shall go
forth, and grow up as
calves of the stall.

MALACHI 4:1,2 KJV

JESUS is the
RIGHTEOUS JUDGE.

He is free from guilt or sin and knows
everything about us. Eternal rewards and
punishments are His to give. JESUS
says . . . My Father looked at Me and
said, This is My beloved Son in whom I
am well pleased. Free yourself now from
any unconfessed sins. As you bring them
to Me, I release you from the penalty and
stand with you so that you receive My
reward . . .

"I have fought the good fight, I have finished the
course, I have kept the faith; in the future there is
laid up for me the crown of righteousness,
which the Lord, the righteous Judge, will
award to me on that day; and not only to
me, but also to all who have loved His
appearing."

II TIMOTHY 4:7,8

JESUS is the
RECEIVER. With
nail-scarred hands, He has taken hold of
power, riches, wisdom, might, honor,
glory, and blessing. All that is God's has
been given to JESUS. He says . . . I
emptied Myself of all my 'rights' so that I
could bring you into fellowship with Me.
In order to receive from Me, you must
first give all to Me. This is a daily
decision. Let all that is within you praise
Me . . .

"For we did not follow cleverly devised tales when we
made known to you the power and coming of our
Lord Jesus Christ, but we were eyewitnesses of
His majesty. For when He received honor
and glory from God the Father, such an
utterance as this was made to Him by
the Majestic Glory, 'This is My
beloved Son with whom I am
well-pleased.' "

II PETER 1:16–17

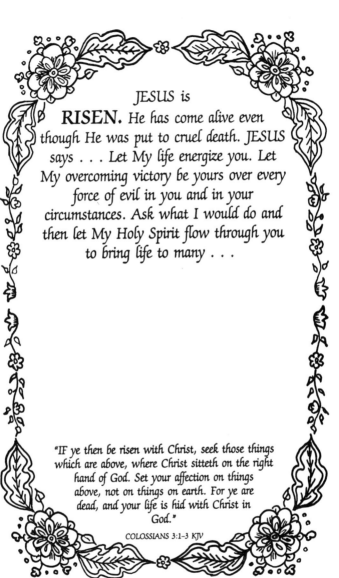

JESUS is

RISEN. He has come alive even though He was put to cruel death. JESUS says . . . Let My life energize you. Let My overcoming victory be yours over every force of evil in you and in your circumstances. Ask what I would do and then let My Holy Spirit flow through you to bring life to many . . .

"IF ye then be risen with Christ, seek those things which are above, where Christ sitteth on the right hand of God. Set your affection on things above, not on things on earth. For ye are dead, and your life is hid with Christ in God."

COLOSSIANS 3:1–3 KJV

JESUS is the
SPIRITUAL ROCK.
Through Him came God's provision for His people in the wilderness. JESUS says . . . Even as I gave Israel water to drink from an impossible source, so will living waters stream from the hard places in your life, if you look to Me . . .

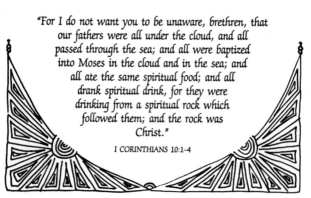

"For I do not want you to be unaware, brethren, that our fathers were all under the cloud, and all passed through the sea; and all were baptized into Moses in the cloud and in the sea; and all ate the same spiritual food; and all drank spiritual drink, for they were drinking from a spiritual rock which followed them; and the rock was Christ."

I CORINTHIANS 10:1-4

JESUS is the
REWARDER. He
pays us wages according to our service,
good or bad. JESUS says . . . The one
who loves Me, cheerfully gives of time,
talent, and self to Me. Visit Me in prison
or in nursing homes, clothe Me, feed Me,
touch My diseased body or tormented
mind with healing, give Me a home. As
you serve others you will find that I have
taken a towel and water to wash your
tired feet . . .

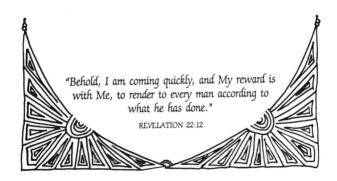

"Behold, I am coming quickly, and My reward is
with Me, to render to every man according to
what he has done."

REVELATION 22:12

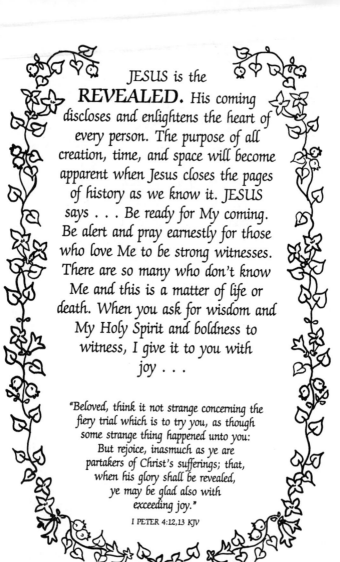

JESUS is the
REVEALED. His coming
discloses and enlightens the heart of
every person. The purpose of all
creation, time, and space will become
apparent when Jesus closes the pages
of history as we know it. JESUS
says . . . Be ready for My coming.
Be alert and pray earnestly for those
who love Me to be strong witnesses.
There are so many who don't know
Me and this is a matter of life or
death. When you ask for wisdom and
My Holy Spirit and boldness to
witness, I give it to you with
joy . . .

"Beloved, think it not strange concerning the
fiery trial which is to try you, as though
some strange thing happened unto you:
But rejoice, inasmuch as ye are
partakers of Christ's sufferings; that,
when his glory shall be revealed,
ye may be glad also with
exceeding joy."

I PETER 4:12,13 KJV

JESUS is the
RESTORER. He brings
us back home again. JESUS
says . . . Just as the Gadarene
demoniac was restored to his right
mind, so My healing Presence brings
you to a better place than you were
in before, cleansed of evil and filled
with My good, My purpose, My
direction for your life . . .

"THE LORD is my shepherd, I shall not
want. He makes me lie down in green
pastures; He leads me beside quiet waters.
He restores my soul; He guides me in
the paths of righteousness For His
name's sake."

PSALM 23:1–3

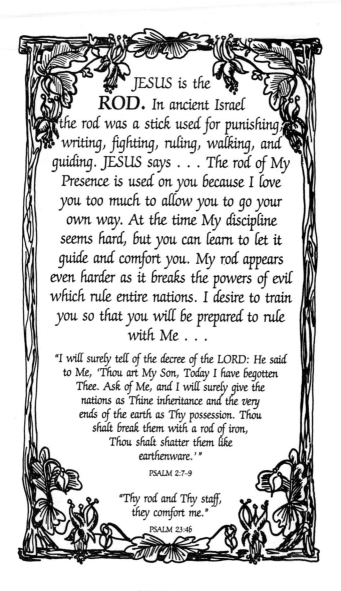

JESUS is the **ROD.** In ancient Israel the rod was a stick used for punishing, writing, fighting, ruling, walking, and guiding. JESUS says . . . The rod of My Presence is used on you because I love you too much to allow you to go your own way. At the time My discipline seems hard, but you can learn to let it guide and comfort you. My rod appears even harder as it breaks the powers of evil which rule entire nations. I desire to train you so that you will be prepared to rule with Me . . .

"I will surely tell of the decree of the LORD: He said to Me, 'Thou art My Son, Today I have begotten Thee. Ask of Me, and I will surely give the nations as Thine inheritance and the very ends of the earth as Thy possession. Thou shalt break them with a rod of iron, Thou shalt shatter them like earthenware.'"

PSALM 2:7–9

"Thy rod and Thy staff, they comfort me."

PSALM 23:46

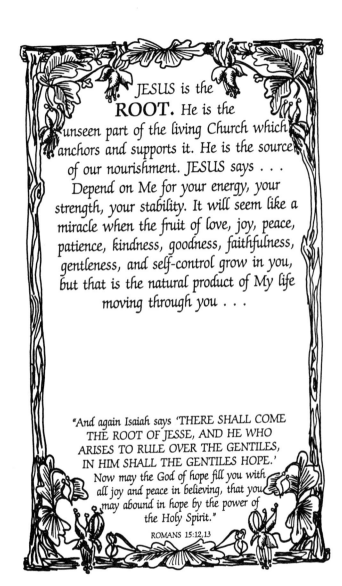

JESUS is the **ROOT.** He is the unseen part of the living Church which anchors and supports it. He is the source of our nourishment. JESUS says . . . Depend on Me for your energy, your strength, your stability. It will seem like a miracle when the fruit of love, joy, peace, patience, kindness, goodness, faithfulness, gentleness, and self-control grow in you, but that is the natural product of My life moving through you . . .

"And again Isaiah says 'THERE SHALL COME THE ROOT OF JESSE, AND HE WHO ARISES TO RULE OVER THE GENTILES, IN HIM SHALL THE GENTILES HOPE.' Now may the God of hope fill you with all joy and peace in believing, that you may abound in hope by the power of the Holy Spirit."

ROMANS 15:12,13

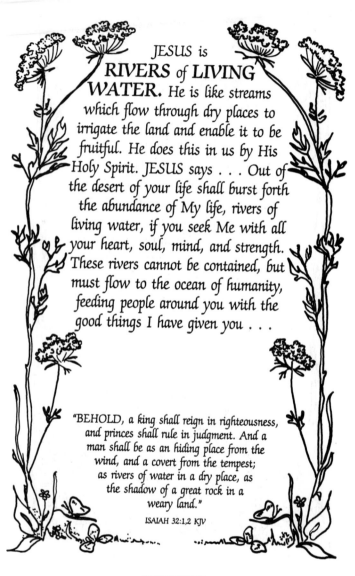

JESUS is
RIVERS of **LIVING
WATER.** He is like streams
which flow through dry places to
irrigate the land and enable it to be
fruitful. He does this in us by His
Holy Spirit. JESUS says . . . Out of
the desert of your life shall burst forth
the abundance of My life, rivers of
living water, if you seek Me with all
your heart, soul, mind, and strength.
These rivers cannot be contained, but
must flow to the ocean of humanity,
feeding people around you with the
good things I have given you . . .

"BEHOLD, a king shall reign in righteousness,
and princes shall rule in judgment. And a
man shall be as an hiding place from the
wind, and a covert from the tempest;
as rivers of water in a dry place, as
the shadow of a great rock in a
weary land."

ISAIAH 32:1,2 KJV

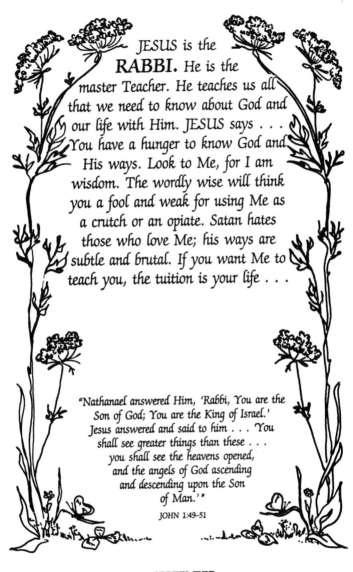

JESUS is the **RABBI.** He is the master Teacher. He teaches us all that we need to know about God and our life with Him. JESUS says . . . You have a hunger to know God and His ways. Look to Me, for I am wisdom. The wordly wise will think you a fool and weak for using Me as a crutch or an opiate. Satan hates those who love Me; his ways are subtle and brutal. If you want Me to teach you, the tuition is your life . . .

"Nathanael answered Him, 'Rabbi, You are the Son of God; You are the King of Israel.' Jesus answered and said to him . . . 'You shall see greater things than these . . . you shall see the heavens opened, and the angels of God ascending and descending upon the Son of Man.'"

JOHN 1:49–51

JESUS is our
SPRING of JOY.
He is a fountain of pure, refreshing,
satisfying gladness which wells up within
us and cannot help but flow out to
others. JESUS says . . . I am in you so
the source of joy is yours. Praise Me even
if it is difficult. Work through the
negative until you see Me in your
situation. Come deeper into your source
and be filled with contagious delight . . .

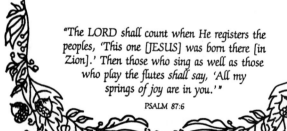

"The LORD shall count when He registers the
peoples, 'This one [JESUS] was born there [in
Zion].' Then those who sing as well as those
who play the flutes shall say, 'All my
springs of joy are in you.'"

PSALM 87:6

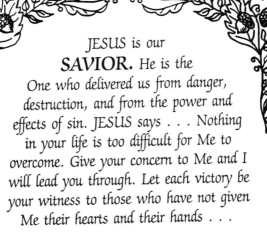

JESUS is our **SAVIOR.** He is the One who delivered us from danger, destruction, and from the power and effects of sin. JESUS says . . . Nothing in your life is too difficult for Me to overcome. Give your concern to Me and I will lead you through. Let each victory be your witness to those who have not given Me their hearts and their hands . . .

"For God has not given us a spirit of timidity [or fear], but of power and love and discipline. Therefore, do not be ashamed of the testimony of our Lord, or of me His prisoner; but join with *me* in suffering for the gospel according to the power of God, who has saved us, and called us with a holy calling, not according to our works, but according to His own purpose and grace . . . revealed by the appearing of our Savior, Christ Jesus."

II TIMOTHY 1:7-10a

JESUS is our
SPRING RAIN.

He is the abundant goodness of God
which waters the late-sown crops. JESUS
says . . . As the ground is still and
allows the rain to refresh it and to soak
into it, I desire you to be still before Me.
Drink in My love and acceptance of you.
To your amazement you will produce
delicious nourishing fruit for many . . .

"COME, let us return to the LORD. For He has
torn us, but He will heal us; He has wounded us,
but He will bandage us. He will revive us after
two days; will raise us up on the third day
that we may live before Him. So let us
know, let us press on to know the
LORD. His going forth is as certain
as the dawn; And He will come
to us like the rain, Like the
spring rain watering the
earth."

HOSEA 6:1–3

JESUS is
SWEETER than honey.
He is the Word of God which is pleasant
to our taste. When He lives in us, we
become the fragrance of life to those who
seek Him. JESUS says . . . You have
grown accustomed to many artificially
sweetened things so your taste is dull.
Look to Me for the natural sweetness
which satisfies . . .

"How sweet are Thy words to my taste! *Yes,*
sweeter than honey to my mouth! From Thy
precepts I get understanding; Therefore, I hate
every false way."

PSALM 119:103,104

JESUS is
SPIRIT. JESUS and the Spirit
of God are one single person and one
perfect united power, victorious over
sickness, demons, sin, and death. JESUS
says . . . Ask for My Spirit to fill you.
Search for My Spirit till you find flowing
through you the boldness, liberty, and
healing My disciples knew. Knock, and
believe Me, the door will be opened for
you . . .

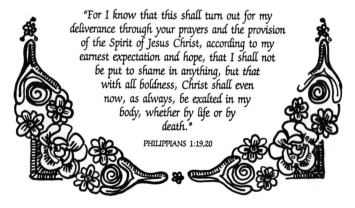

"For I know that this shall turn out for my
deliverance through your prayers and the provision
of the Spirit of Jesus Christ, according to my
earnest expectation and hope, that I shall not
be put to shame in anything, but that
with all boldness, Christ shall even
now, as always, be exalted in my
body, whether by life or by
death."

PHILIPPIANS 1:19,20

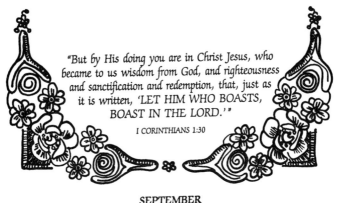

JESUS is our

SANCTIFICATION.

He is our purifier, the One who makes us holy. JESUS says . . . You have come into My Body, the Church, by My blood poured out for you. You are set apart with your brothers and sisters in Me for God's use. Walk in My steps and let Me cherish and nourish you. You will find the old lusts disappear. All your heights and depths will fit into My plan which completes you . . .

"But by His doing you are in Christ Jesus, who became to us wisdom from God, and righteousness and sanctification and redemption, that, just as it is written, 'LET HIM WHO BOASTS, BOAST IN THE LORD.'"

I CORINTHIANS 1:30

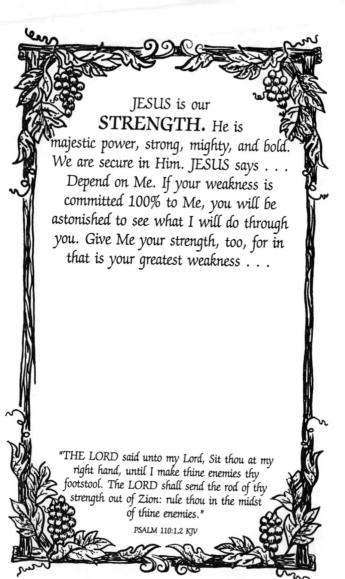

JESUS is our
STRENGTH. He is
majestic power, strong, mighty, and bold.
We are secure in Him. JESUS says . . .
Depend on Me. If your weakness is
committed 100% to Me, you will be
astonished to see what I will do through
you. Give Me your strength, too, for in
that is your greatest weakness . . .

"THE LORD said unto my Lord, Sit thou at my
right hand, until I make thine enemies thy
footstool. The LORD shall send the rod of thy
strength out of Zion: rule thou in the midst
of thine enemies."

PSALM 110:1,2 KJV

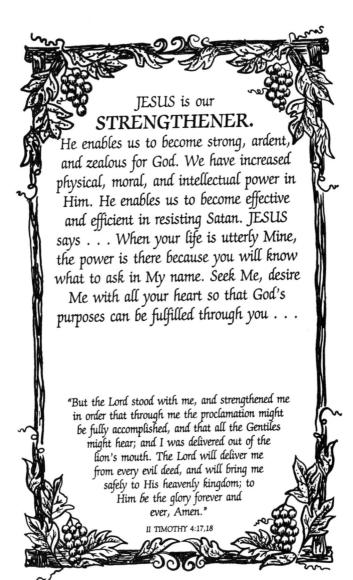

JESUS is our
STRENGTHENER.

He enables us to become strong, ardent,
and zealous for God. We have increased
physical, moral, and intellectual power in
Him. He enables us to become effective
and efficient in resisting Satan. JESUS
says . . . When your life is utterly Mine,
the power is there because you will know
what to ask in My name. Seek Me, desire
Me with all your heart so that God's
purposes can be fulfilled through you . . .

"But the Lord stood with me, and strengthened me
in order that through me the proclamation might
be fully accomplished, and that all the Gentiles
might hear; and I was delivered out of the
lion's mouth. The Lord will deliver me
from every evil deed, and will bring me
safely to His heavenly kingdom; to
Him be the glory forever and
ever, Amen."

II TIMOTHY 4:17,18

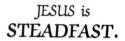

JESUS is
STEADFAST.

He turned resolutely in the direction of the
cross and stayed on that path until it was
finished. JESUS says . . . God requires of
you a choice and a determination to stick
to that choice no matter how difficult the
way becomes. I will be with you and help
you. No matter how many times Satan
pushes you, or you stumble and fall, keep
on that narrow path. Even if it leads you
through death, it is the only way of
life . . .

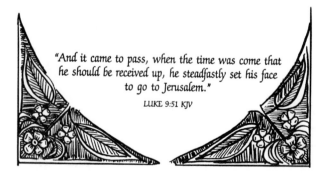

"And it came to pass, when the time was come that
he should be received up, he steadfastly set his face
to go to Jerusalem."

LUKE 9:51 KJV

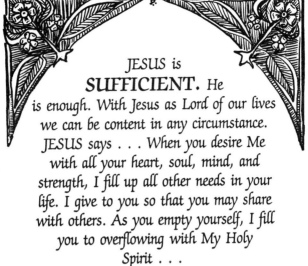

JESUS is
SUFFICIENT. He
is enough. With Jesus as Lord of our lives
we can be content in any circumstance.
JESUS says . . . When you desire Me
with all your heart, soul, mind, and
strength, I fill up all other needs in your
life. I give to you so that you may share
with others. As you empty yourself, I fill
you to overflowing with My Holy
Spirit . . .

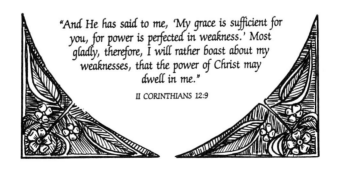

"And He has said to me, 'My grace is sufficient for
you, for power is perfected in weakness.' Most
gladly, therefore, I will rather boast about my
weaknesses, that the power of Christ may
dwell in me."

II CORINTHIANS 12:9

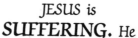

JESUS is
SUFFERING. He
experienced hardship and pain in His
birth, life, and death. Even now He feels
with us, His Body, as we pay the terrible
price of death to ourselves and become
vulnerable to persecution for His name.
JESUS says . . . Have you lost blood
because you bear My name? When this
happens you can know if you truly stand
with Me. Meanwhile, trust Me to enable
you to overcome in the daily little things
and pray for those who are suffering
persecution today . . .

"Beloved, do not be surprised at the fiery ordeal
among you, which comes upon you for your
testing, as though some strange thing were
happening to you; but to the degree that you
share the sufferings of Christ, keep on
rejoicing; so that also at the revelation
of His glory, you may rejoice with
exultation."

I PETER 4:12,13

JESUS is
STRONG. He is
powerful, mighty, and valiant. Jesus is
able to keep what we have committed into
His care. He says . . . The world
magnifies the power of Satan and thrills
at his evil works while I am portrayed as
an ineffectual sissy in a bathrobe. Let Me
be in you all that I AM and you will see
those lies crumble. You will see that in
you I am greater than all the forces of
darkness . . .

"When a strong *man* fully armed guards his own
homestead, his possessions are undisturbed; but
when someone stronger than he attacks him
and overpowers him, he takes away from
him all his armor on whch he had relied,
and distributes his plunder. He who is
not with Me is against Me."

LUKE 11:21–23a

JESUS is the
STANDARD. He is
the flag, the banner which is lifted up
over the people of God. Under Him we
rally. He leads us by the example of His
death to self on the cross. JESUS
says . . . I did not choose to glorify
Myself. I did not choose to die for you. I
was chosen and let God have His way.
What is God calling you to today? As you
lift Me up, acknowledging My way as the
one, true way, you will receive strength to
move into whatever battles Satan brings
against you and overcome . . .

"Go through, go through the gates; Clear the way for
the people; Build up, build up the highway;
Remove the stones, lift up a standard over the
peoples. Behold, the LORD has proclaimed
to the end of the earth, say to the
daughter of Zion, 'Lo your salvation
comes; Behold His reward is with
Him, and His recompense before
Him.' "

ISAIAH 62:10,11

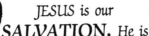

JESUS is our
SALVATION. He is
our deliverance from the evil one, and
from sin and its effects. He is our health.
JESUS says . . . To love Me is to know
Me and to take into yourself the powerful,
positive force of resurrection life. It is My
nature to renew and restore your body,
mind, and spirit; expect this. Such glory
cannot be contained in one earthly vessel
but must spill over and pour itself out for
all who are thirsty . . .

"And there is salvation in no one else; for there is no
other name under heaven that has been given
among men, by which we must be saved."

ACTS 4:12

JESUS is a
POLISHED SHAFT.

His Word is swift, direct, penetrating. As a sharp, smooth, gleaming sword in its sheath or arrow in its quiver awaits the perfect timing of its owner to come out of its hidden place to pierce the heart, so Jesus waited until God's time had come. JESUS says . . . There is a time for you to immerse yourself in My Word and a time to wait in the Presence of God. He will direct you when it is time to go out and to speak, to publish the good news. Let My patience and humility work in you, for those proclaiming Me publicly will be persecuted . . .

"And he hath made my mouth like a sharp sword; in the shadow of his hand hath he hid me, and made me a polished shaft; in his quiver hath he hid me; And said unto me, Thou art my servant, O Israel, in whom I will be glorified."

ISAIAH 49:2,3 KJV

JESUS is the
SECOND MAN. He
is the second Adam, the resurrected,
glorified Man who makes us radiantly
alive. The first man, Adam, through his
earthiness brought sin, condemnation and
death to all people. JESUS says . . .

Consider this: Vibrant, abundant,
victorious life is yours in Me. In Me you
become part of this second man. In Me
Satan's lies, diseases, and death have been
overcome. Place your problem, your needs
in My hand so that I can demonstrate My
power available for you today . . .

"So also it is written, 'The first MAN, ADAM,
BECAME A LIVING SOUL.' The last Adam became a
life-giving spirit. However, the spiritual is not first, but
the natural; then the spiritual. The first man is from
the earth, earthy; the second man is from heaven. As is
the earthy; so also are those who are earthy; and as is
the heavenly, so also are those who are heavenly. And
just as we have borne the image of the earthy, we shall
also bear the image of the heavenly.' "

I CORINTHIANS 15:45–49

JESUS is a
SWEET SAVOUR.
It is Jesus' total gift of Himself to God
which is a delight, a pleasure to God. It
is the distinctive aroma of the sacrificial
love which God Himself had for us in
giving us His Son. JESUS says . . . You
are the salt in the stew of the earth's
peoples. You are the flavoring which is
essential, which makes life bearable, even
enjoyable. When others recognize in you
the sweetness of My Presence, they will
respond. They will taste and see that I
am good . . .

"BE ye therefore followers of God, as dear children:
And walk in love, as Christ also hath loved us,
and hath given himself for us an offering and a
sacrifice to God for a sweet–smelling savour."

EPHESIANS 5:1–2 KJV

JESUS is our **SURETY.** He is God's pledge, our legal assurance that the new agreement with God will be fulfilled. We can have confidence, certainty, and depend on the ability of Jesus to cleanse us and draw us close to God. JESUS says . . . Nothing you have ever done can separate you from My love for you. Do not continue in your sin, but hate it with passion. My love is like a sharp knife which cuts away the rottenness to release and preserve the good fruit . . .

" . . . The Lord sware and will not repent, Thou art a priest for ever after the order of Mel-chis-ed-ec: By so much was Jesus made a surety of a better testament . . . because he continueth ever, hath an unchangeable priesthood. Wherefore he is able also to save them to the uttermost that come unto God by him, seeing he ever liveth to make intercession for them."

HEBREWS 7:21b–22,24–25 KJV

JESUS is the
SON of **DAVID.** He is the Promised
One to continue the glorious reign of King
David. His Kingdom is one of freedom,
glory, righteousness, and peace. JESUS
says . . . Open to Me the throne of your
heart. I am King; let Me reign
triumphantly in you. With the eagerness
and innocent faith of the boy David,
together we will be God's chosen
instrument to overcome the giants in the
land . . .

"And as Jesus passed on from there, two blind men
followed Him, crying out, and saying, 'Have
mercy on us, Son of David!' . . . Jesus said to
them, 'Do you believe that I am able to do
this?' They said to Him, 'Yes, Lord.'
Then He touched their eyes, saying,
'Be it done to you according to your
faith.' And their eyes were
opened."

MATTHEW 9:27,28b–30a

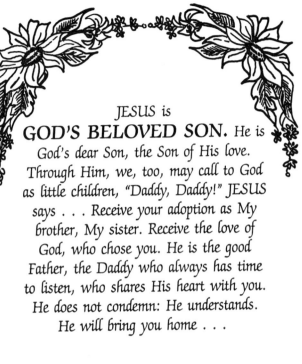

JESUS is
GOD'S BELOVED SON.
He is God's dear Son, the Son of His love. Through Him, we, too, may call to God as little children, "Daddy, Daddy!" JESUS says . . . Receive your adoption as My brother, My sister. Receive the love of God, who chose you. He is the good Father, the Daddy who always has time to listen, who shares His heart with you. He does not condemn: He understands. He will bring you home . . .

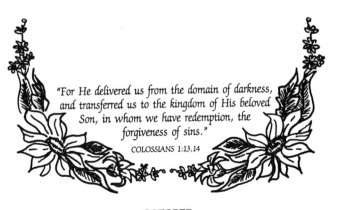

"For He delivered us from the domain of darkness, and transferred us to the kingdom of His beloved Son, in whom we have redemption, the forgiveness of sins."

COLOSSIANS 1:13,14

JESUS is the
SON of **GOD.** He accepted the title
because His nature and attributes are the
same as God's. He is co-equal and co-
eternal with God. JESUS says . . . I
have called you to be part of My family.
As you enjoy the benefits of knowing God
as your Daddy and Me as your big
brother, you will take on the family
characteristics, more and more. When you
see good things in yourself, praise Me, for
you are growing up to be just like your
Dad. I am doing it in you . . .

"But Jesus kept silent. And the high priest said to
Him, 'I adjure You by the living God, that You
tell us whether You are the Christ, the Son of
God.' Jesus said to him, 'You have said it
yourself; nevertheless I tell you, hereafter
you shall see THE SON OF MAN
SITTING ON THE RIGHT
HAND OF POWER, AND
COMING ON THE
CLOUDS OF HEAVEN.' "

MATTHEW 26:63,64

JESUS is the
SON of MAN.
This is the title Jesus used of himself seventy-eight times in the Gospels. With this name Jesus identifies with the despised, the common, the fallen race of man. He is friend of sinners, yet the Son of Man will return with glory as Judge of all. JESUS says . . . What will I find you doing when I return? Ask Me today and each day what I would have you do. I know your capabilities and weaknesses.

I, your Creator, have walked in your shoes. Resist the pressure of the world and of religious forms. Let Me lead . . .

"But when the Son of Man comes in His glory, and all the angels with Him, then He will sit on His glorious throne. And all the nations will be gathered before Him; and He will separate them from one another, as the shepherd separates the sheep from the goats."

MATTHEW 25:31–32

JESUS is the
SUCCOURER.
He comes to the aid of the one in
distress. JESUS says, You cannot hide
from My Presence. David knew from
experience that though he made his bed in
hell, I was there. I walk on the troubled
waters of fear, resentments, rage,
bitterness and say, "Peace, be still." All
the elements within you and without
must obey My voice when you cry. 'Lord,
have mercy!'

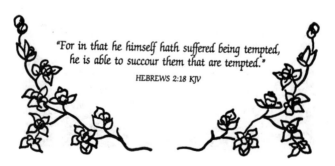

"For in that he himself hath suffered being tempted,
he is able to succour them that are tempted."

HEBREWS 2:18 KJV

JESUS is a
TRIED STONE.

He is the secure foundation which has been tested and found to be trustworthy. JESUS says . . . You are part of My building, the temple which God's glory will fill. Rest on Me. Let the Master Builder work on you with hammer and chisel till you are shaped to fit those stones near you. Let Him melt away impurities with the fire of My Holy Spirit within and the heat of circumstances without. I make you useful . . .

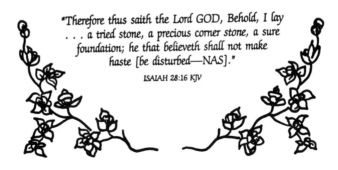

"Therefore thus saith the Lord GOD, Behold, I lay . . . a tried stone, a precious corner stone, a sure foundation; he that believeth shall not make haste [be disturbed—NAS]."

ISAIAH 28:16 KJV

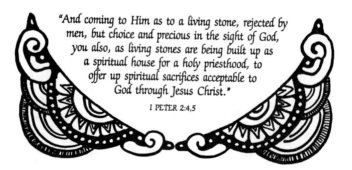

JESUS is a
LIVING STONE.
The resurrected Jesus is the foundation of
all that God is doing. Our strong hearts
are changed by Him to hearts of
compassion so that we can become part of
the place of peace and praise where God
dwells. JESUS says . . . I have chosen
you. As I shape you, keep your eyes on
My purpose for including you. You are
precious to Me. Because I live, you can
live fully in the place where I put
you . . .

"And coming to Him as to a living stone, rejected by
men, but choice and precious in the sight of God,
you also, as living stones are being built up as
a spiritual house for a holy priesthood, to
offer up spiritual sacrifices acceptable to
God through Jesus Christ."

I PETER 2:4,5

JESUS is the
SON of **MARY.** It was God's perfect
plan to favor a virgin daughter of Israel,
from the family of David, the tribe of
Judah, to be the mother of His Son.
Because the Holy Spirit planted God's
seed in her womb, the son of Mary is
also the Son of God. JESUS says . . . I
love My mother, Mary. She was willing
to be used as God's instrument even
though it meant great heartache and
suffering for her. She also knows supreme
joy. Let her attitude be yours: Be it done
to me according to your word.

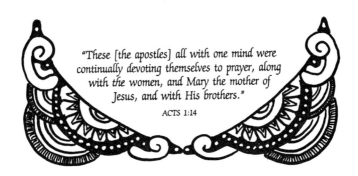

"These [the apostles] all with one mind were
continually devoting themselves to prayer, along
with the women, and Mary the mother of
Jesus, and with His brothers."

ACTS 1:14

JESUS is our
SERVANT. He looks for opportunity
to help and assist us. He freely gives
Himself in order that we may have God's
best. JESUS says, Let Me wash your
feet. After you experience refreshing and
cleansing as the filth and cares of the
world are washed away, you will desire to
do the same for your brothers and sisters
in Me, and for the poor . . .

"It is not so among you, but whoever wishes to
become great among you shall be your servant,
and whoever wishes to be first among you shall
be your slave; just as the Son of Man did
not come to be served, but to serve, and
to give His life a ransom for many."

MATTHEW 20:26-28

JESUS is the
SHEPHERD of OUR SOULS.
Jesus has compassion on us, the sheep in His care. His compassion results in healing of our bodies, souls (our minds and memories), and of our spirits. JESUS says . . . I teach you all you need to know. As I carry you over the rough places in life, you hear the beat of My heart, feel the warmth of My breath. I continually give Myself to enable you to be whole . . .

". . . and He Himself bore our sins in His body on the cross, that we might die to sin and live to righteousness; for by His wounds you were healed. For you were continually straying like sheep, but now you have returned to the Shepherd and Guardian of your souls."

I PETER 2:24,25

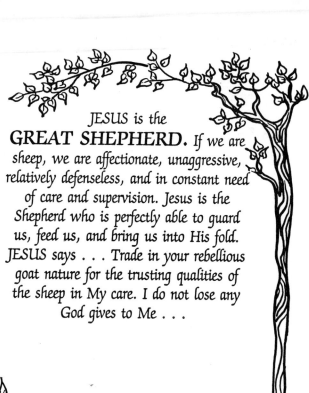

JESUS is the
GREAT SHEPHERD. If we are
sheep, we are affectionate, unaggressive,
relatively defenseless, and in constant need
of care and supervision. Jesus is the
Shepherd who is perfectly able to guard
us, feed us, and bring us into His fold.
JESUS says . . . Trade in your rebellious
goat nature for the trusting qualities of
the sheep in My care. I do not lose any
God gives to Me . . .

"Now the God of peace, who brought up from the
dead the great Shepherd of the sheep through the
blood of the eternal covenant, *even* Jesus our
Lord, equip you in every good thing to do
His will, working in us that which is
pleasing in His sight, through Jesus
Christ, to whom be the glory forever
and ever. Amen."

HEBREWS 13:20,21

OCTOBER
12

JESUS is the
GOOD SHEPHERD.

He gives His life to save, sustain and redeem the life of all who come into His fold, the Jew first and then the Gentile. JESUS says . . . Let Me lead you into the paths of peace. Let Me guide you over rocky and dangerous, death-filled ways to the place where waters are not troubled, where the worst your enemies can do to you will not touch you as you rest and eat at My table . . .

"I am the good shepherd; and I know My own, and My own know Me, even as the Father knows Me and I know the Father; and I lay down My life for the sheep. And I have other sheep, which are not of this fold; I must bring them also, and they shall hear My voice; and they shall become one flock with one shepherd."

JOHN 10:14–16

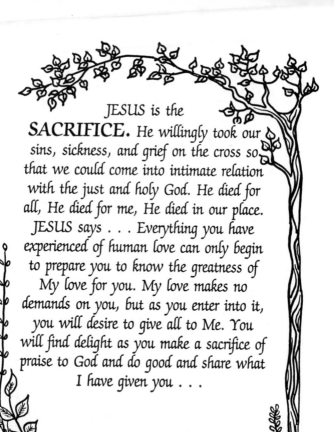

JESUS is the
SACRIFICE. He willingly took our
sins, sickness, and grief on the cross so
that we could come into intimate relation
with the just and holy God. He died for
all, He died for me, He died in our place.
JESUS says . . . Everything you have
experienced of human love can only begin
to prepare you to know the greatness of
My love for you. My love makes no
demands on you, but as you enter into it,
you will desire to give all to Me. You
will find delight as you make a sacrifice of
praise to God and do good and share what
I have given you . . .

"He, having offered one sacrifice for sins for all time,
sat down at the right hand of God, waiting from
that time onward UNTIL HIS ENEMIES BE
MADE A FOOTSTOOL FOR HIS FEET.
For by one offering He has perfected for all
time those who are sanctified."

HEBREWS 10:12–14

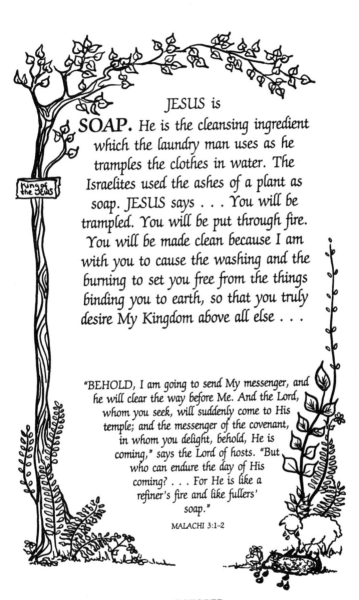

JESUS is

SOAP. He is the cleansing ingredient which the laundry man uses as he tramples the clothes in water. The Israelites used the ashes of a plant as soap. JESUS says . . . You will be trampled. You will be put through fire. You will be made clean because I am with you to cause the washing and the burning to set you free from the things binding you to earth, so that you truly desire My Kingdom above all else . . .

"BEHOLD, I am going to send My messenger, and he will clear the way before Me. And the Lord, whom you seek, will suddenly come to His temple; and the messenger of the covenant, in whom you delight, behold, He is coming," says the Lord of hosts. "But who can endure the day of His coming? . . . For He is like a refiner's fire and like fullers' soap."

MALACHI 3:1–2

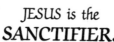

JESUS is the
SANCTIFIER.

He makes us holy, purifies and consecrates us, so that we are able to stand blameless before God as saints. JESUS says . . . I have chosen you to be Mine. Follow Me. This will cost you everything the world holds dear. The gain is everything My Father has. No one can stretch, strain, or strive his way to heaven. No idol, no philosophy, no system of thought will find God, for even as they build Babels, He will confuse them. Follow Me, love Me, for I am the only Way . . .

"As Thou didst send Me into the world, I also have sent them into the world. And for their sakes I sanctify Myself, that they themselves also may be sanctified in truth. I do not ask in behalf of these alone, but for those also who believe in Me through their word; that they may all be one."

JOHN 17:18–21a

JESUS is the
SPRING of WATER. He
is a fountain which pours forth sparkling,
pure, living water in the midst of a dry,
barren land. JESUS says . . . I know all
about you. I know the husbands you have
been living with while you pretend to be
married to Me. Drink from My well
instead of building for yourself reservoirs
which are cracked and broken. Drink
deeply of Me and you will become a
reservoir which will bear life-giving water
in abundant supply to those around
you . . .

"Take courage, fear not. Behold, your God will come
with vengeance; The recompense of God will come,
But He will save you. Then the eyes of the blind
will be opened, And the ears of the deaf will be
unstopped. Then the lame will leap like a deer, And
the tongue of the dumb will shout for joy. For waters
will break forth in the wilderness And streams in the
Arabah. And the scorched land will become a
pool, And the thirsty ground springs of water."

ISAIAH 35:4b–7a

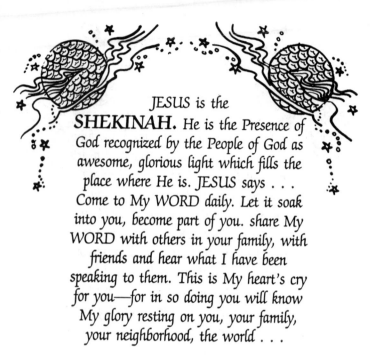

JESUS is the **SHEKINAH.** He is the Presence of God recognized by the People of God as awesome, glorious light which fills the place where He is. JESUS says . . . Come to My WORD daily. Let it soak into you, become part of you. share My WORD with others in your family, with friends and hear what I have been speaking to them. This is My heart's cry for you—for in so doing you will know My glory resting on you, your family, your neighborhood, the world . . .

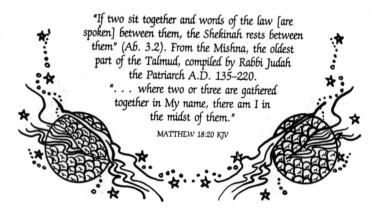

"If two sit together and words of the law [are spoken] between them, the Shekinah rests between them" (Ab. 3.2). From the Mishna, the oldest part of the Talmud, compiled by Rabbi Judah the Patriarch A.D. 135–220.

". . . where two or three are gathered together in My name, there am I in the midst of them."

MATTHEW 18:20 KJV

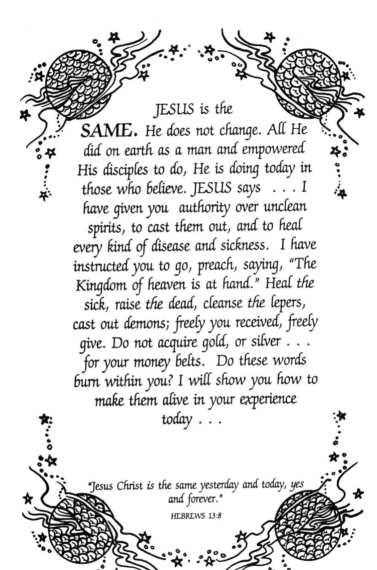

JESUS is the
SAME. He does not change. All He
did on earth as a man and empowered
His disciples to do, He is doing today in
those who believe. JESUS says . . . I
have given you authority over unclean
spirits, to cast them out, and to heal
every kind of disease and sickness. I have
instructed you to go, preach, saying, "The
Kingdom of heaven is at hand." Heal the
sick, raise the dead, cleanse the lepers,
cast out demons; freely you received, freely
give. Do not acquire gold, or silver . . .
for your money belts. Do these words
burn within you? I will show you how to
make them alive in your experience
today . . .

"Jesus Christ is the same yesterday and today, yes
and forever."

HEBREWS 13:8

JESUS is the
SHILOH. He is the "Giver of Peace,"
"Rest," the "Sent One," "He whose right
it is." Jacob foresaw in a prophetic vision
that through Judah would come the
Shiloh, the Messiah, the One God would
send as King over all peoples. He would
enable people to be what God created
them to be. JESUS says . . . I have come
to rule, to take over your life. Only by
submitting to My ways will you find rest,
peace, and fulfillment. Put down all
rebellions and insurrections within you so
that you may know My victory . . .

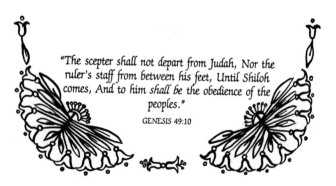

"The scepter shall not depart from Judah, Nor the
ruler's staff from between his feet, Until Shiloh
comes, And to him *shall* be the obedience of the
peoples."

GENESIS 49:10

JESUS is the **SUN SHINING** in its **STRENGTH.** In His presence there is no need for the light of a lamp or the light of the sun, because in Him there is no darkness, only radiance, warmth, and a continual burning. JESUS says . . . You are the light of the world. Let your light shine before men in such a way that they see your good works. All the gifts and abilities I give you, all that I am inside you—my love, joy, and peace— will shine out through your eyes, mouth, and what you do so that those around you may have reason to praise God. Let Me shine through you today . . .

" . . . and in the middle of the lampstands one like a son of man, clothed in a robe reaching to the feet, and girded across His breast with a golden girdle. . . . And in His right hand He held seven stars; and out of His mouth came a sharp two-edged sword; and His face was like the sun shining in its strength."

REVELATION 1:13,16

JESUS is the
SHADE. He gives shelter, protection, rest, and refreshing in the midst of a dry, parched, barren, and weary land. JESUS says . . . Underneath the glitter and glamor of materialistic and mechanized society lies a valley of dry bones bleached by the penetrating light of God's presence. I am the sun which exposes the emptiness and decay. I am also the shade which protects all those who seek Me with all their hearts. Come to Me without fear, with openness. I am gentle in My cleansing. I am eager to give you resurrection life . . .

"When the LORD has washed away the filth of the daughters of Zion, and purged the bloodshed of Jerusalem from her midst, by the spirit of judgment and the spirit of burning, then the LORD will create . . . over her assemblies a cloud by day, even smoke, and the brightness of a flaming fire by night . . . And there will be a shelter to give shade from the heat by day, and refuge and protection from the storm and the rain."

ISAIAH 4:4–6

OCTOBER
22

JESUS is the
SOWER. He has scattered His people
as good seed over the earth so that there
will be a good harvest for God's
Kingdom. It is the sower's responsibility
to have the weeds uprooted and burned.
JESUS says . . . I chose you, I planted
you, I care for your growth. Don't let
worry about evil around you cause you to
lash out, to criticize, to use the enemy's
tactics to destroy. Let the good fruit of
love, joy, peace, patience, kindness,
gentleness grow in you. Be part of My
solution, God's Kingdom . . .

"The one who sows the good seed is the Son of
Man, and the field is the world; and as for the
good seed, these are the sons of the kingdom;
and the tares are the sons of the evil one;
and the enemy who sowed them is the
devil, and the harvest is the end of the
age; and the reapers are angels."

MATTHEW 13:37b–39

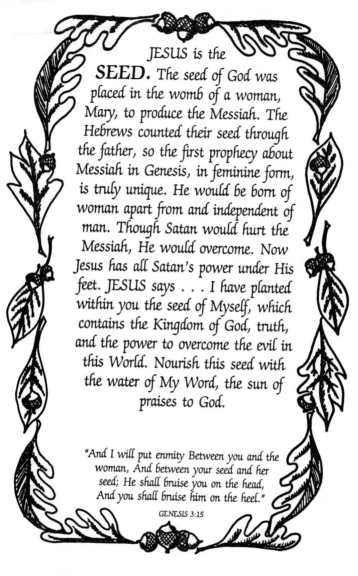

JESUS is the
SEED. The seed of God was placed in the womb of a woman, Mary, to produce the Messiah. The Hebrews counted their seed through the father, so the first prophecy about Messiah in Genesis, in feminine form, is truly unique. He would be born of woman apart from and independent of man. Though Satan would hurt the Messiah, He would overcome. Now Jesus has all Satan's power under His feet. JESUS says . . . I have planted within you the seed of Myself, which contains the Kingdom of God, truth, and the power to overcome the evil in this World. Nourish this seed with the water of My Word, the sun of praises to God.

"And I will put enmity Between you and the woman, And between your seed and her seed; He shall bruise you on the head, And you shall bruise him on the heel."

GENESIS 3:15

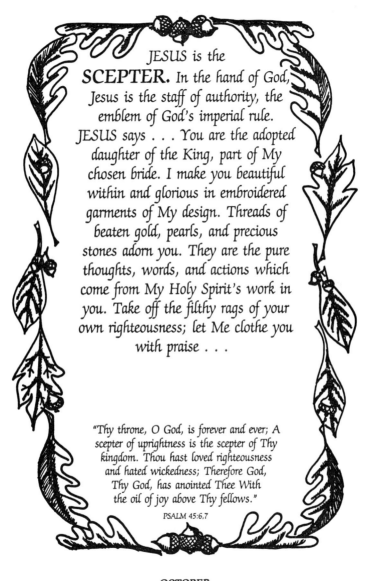

JESUS is the

SCEPTER. In the hand of God, Jesus is the staff of authority, the emblem of God's imperial rule. JESUS says . . . You are the adopted daughter of the King, part of My chosen bride. I make you beautiful within and glorious in embroidered garments of My design. Threads of beaten gold, pearls, and precious stones adorn you. They are the pure thoughts, words, and actions which come from My Holy Spirit's work in you. Take off the filthy rags of your own righteousness; let Me clothe you with praise . . .

"Thy throne, O God, is forever and ever; A scepter of uprightness is the scepter of Thy kingdom. Thou hast loved righteousness and hated wickedness; Therefore God, Thy God, has anointed Thee With the oil of joy above Thy fellows."

PSALM 45:6,7

OCTOBER
25

JESUS is the
SIGN. He is the baby born to a virgin foretold by Isaiah, a sign of God's care for Israel. He is the sign of Jonah; He was buried three days and lives again. JESUS says . . . When in new territory you carefully follow the signs to find your direction. On your journey into the fullness of God's Kingdom, keep your eyes on Me, follow Me, obey Me, trust Me. I am the sign that loves you . . .

"And the angel said to them, 'Do not be afraid; for behold, I bring you good news of a great joy which shall be for all the people; for today in the city of David there has been born for you a Savior, who is Christ the Lord. And this *will* be a sign for you: you will find a baby wrapped in cloths, and lying in a manger.' "

LUKE 2:10-12

JESUS is the
BLAZING STAR. He is a shining
Prince who rules over the nations; He
gives that authority to those who
overcome. JESUS says . . . I, Jesus, have
sent My angel to testify to you these
things for the churches. I am the root and
the offspring of David, the bright morning
star. And the Spirit and the bride say,
"Come." And let the one who is thirsty
come; let the one who wishes take the
water of life without cost . . .

*"I see him, but not now; I behold him, but not near;
A star shall come forth from Jacob, And a scepter
shall rise from Israel, And shall crush through
the forehead of Moab, And tear down all the
sons of Sheth [i.e., Tumult]."*

NUMBERS 24:17

OCTOBER
27

JESUS is the
NEW SONG. He is the fresh
beginning of a melody, a poetical chant, a
cantillation of superior quality to all
previous songs. JESUS says . . . The
prophet Zephaniah foretold "The LORD
thy God in the midst of thee is mighty;
he will save, he will rejoice over thee
with joy; he will rest in his love, he will
joy over thee with singing" (Zephaniah
3:17 KJV). In John's revelation you can
see the angels and apostles joining in the
song. I am the music. I am the song.
Learn your part and sing in harmony with
the hosts in the heavenlies . . .

"And when He had taken the book, the four living
creatures and the twenty-four elders fell down before the
Lamb, having each one a harp, and golden bowls full of
incense, which are the prayers of the saints. And they
sang a new song, saying, 'Worthy art Thou to take the
book, and to break its seals; for Thou wast slain, and
didst purchase for God with Thy blood men from
every tribe and tongue and people and nation.
And Thou hast made them to be a
kingdom and priests
to our God.' "

REVELATION 5:8–10

OCTOBER
28

JESUS is the
SEEKER. In obedience to God and as an act of worship, Jesus earnestly desires and searches for each person who has lost the way to his heavenly home. JESUS says . . . Long have I searched for you on wilderness paths to bring you into My arms. I have others who are out there bleating because they are afraid and can't find the way. Will you leave the safety of the fold and go with Me to find them?

"For the Son of man is come to save that which was lost. How think ye? if a man have an hundred sheep, and one of them be gone astray, doth he not leave the ninety and nine, and goeth into the mountains, and seeketh that which is gone astray? And if so be that he find it . . . he rejoiceth more of that sheep, than of the ninety and nine which went not astray."

MATTHEW 18:11–13 KJV

JESUS is the

SANCTUARY. He is the consecrated, holy place where God dwells and where we can go for safety. JESUS says . . . In the midst of an earth where evil seems to reign unchecked, in the very place where you are ridiculed for your beliefs in Me, even persecuted for My name, you can sanctify Me in your heart. I will be to you a sanctuary. In the midst of your enemies you can sit with My Father, commune, and enjoy the banquet, as you rest in Me, the holiest place . . .

"It is the LORD of hosts whom you should regard as holy. And He shall be your fear, And He shall be your dread. Then He shall become a sanctuary; But to both the houses of Israel, a stone to strike and a rock to stumble over."

ISAIAH 8:13,14a

JESUS is the
SON of the **LIVING GOD.** In the
Old Testament, the living God is
frequently contrasted with powerless,
insensitive idols made of stone. In Jesus
we see all of God's compassion and ability
to overcome evil with good. JESUS
says . . . Choose today whom you will
serve, the living God who loves you or
the false gods of this world. You were
created for the love I have for you, and
only when you die to self and live in My
love will you be truly happy . . .

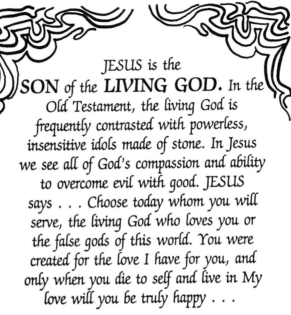

"He said to them, 'But who do you say that I am?'
And Simon Peter answered and said, 'Thou art
the Christ, the Son of the living God.' And
Jesus answered and said to him, 'Blessed are
you Simon Barjona, because flesh and
blood did not reveal this to you, but
My Father who is in heaven.'"

MATTHEW 16:15–17

OCTOBER
31

JESUS is a
STRANGER. He was looked on as a
foreigner, as one who was different, an
intruder into accepted Jewish culture of
2000 years ago. His own people threw
him out of town, His own brothers did
not believe in Him. The religious leaders
considered Him dangerous and plotted His
death. JESUS says . . . Father, forgive
them was My cry even as I was dying
on the cross. Let this attitude be yours
toward those who hate you. As I live in
you, you can feel what it means to
overcome rejection with forgiveness. It
will cause you to welcome strangers in
your midst, even as you welcome Me . . .

"For I was hungry, and you gave Me something to
eat; I was thirsty, and you gave Me drink; I was
a stranger, and you invited Me in."

MATTHEW 25:35

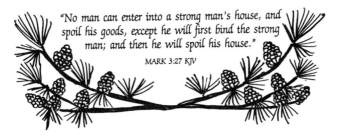

JESUS is the **SPOILER** of Satan's house. He went through death into hell and brought out those people of God who had longed for His coming. Today He enters Satan's kingdom to rescue those who are bound and have been robbed of salvation. JESUS says . . . I have given you authority, as My disciples, to bind that strong man, Satan, and to plunder his house of the precious ones he has stolen from Me. I give you [plural] discernment to know what chains bind them. I give you power to break those chains and to loose the Holy Spirit's qualities in their lives. In prayer we can help them want release.

"No man can enter into a strong man's house, and spoil his goods, except he will first bind the strong man; and then he will spoil his house."

MARK 3:27 KJV

JESUS is the **STUMBLING STONE.** Faith in the Christ crucified is to Jews a stumbling block and to Gentiles, foolishness. In Him we are called, not to religious forms and works, but to love one another. JESUS says . . . Look to Me. I give you the faith to keep from stumbling. I give you the love and forgiveness you need for your brothers and sisters and for a lost, lonely world. My love is yours . . .

"Gentiles, who did not pursue righteousness, attained righteousness, even the righteousness which is by faith, but Israel, pursuing a law of righteousness, did not arrive at that law. Why? Because they did not pursue it by faith but as though it were by works. They stumbled over THE STUMBLING STONE, just as it is written, 'BEHOLD, I LAY IN ZION A STONE OF STUMBLING AND A ROCK OF OFFENSE. AND HE WHO BELIEVES IN HIM WILL NOT BE DISAPPOINTED.'"

ROMANS 9:30–33

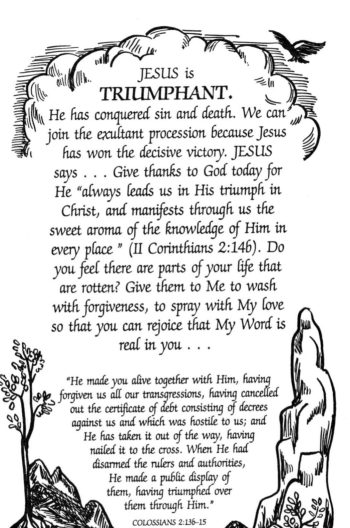

JESUS is
TRIUMPHANT.

He has conquered sin and death. We can join the exultant procession because Jesus has won the decisive victory. JESUS says . . . Give thanks to God today for He "always leads us in His triumph in Christ, and manifests through us the sweet aroma of the knowledge of Him in every place" (II Corinthians 2:14b). Do you feel there are parts of your life that are rotten? Give them to Me to wash with forgiveness, to spray with My love so that you can rejoice that My Word is real in you . . .

"He made you alive together with Him, having forgiven us all our transgressions, having cancelled out the certificate of debt consisting of decrees against us and which was hostile to us; and He has taken it out of the way, having nailed it to the cross. When He had disarmed the rulers and authorities, He made a public display of them, having triumphed over them through Him."

COLOSSIANS 2:13b–15

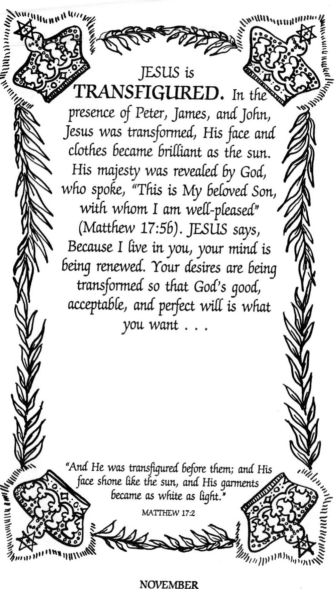

JESUS is
TRANSFIGURED. In the
presence of Peter, James, and John,
Jesus was transformed, His face and
clothes became brilliant as the sun.
His majesty was revealed by God,
who spoke, "This is My beloved Son,
with whom I am well-pleased"
(Matthew 17:5b). JESUS says,
Because I live in you, your mind is
being renewed. Your desires are being
transformed so that God's good,
acceptable, and perfect will is what
you want . . .

"And He was transfigured before them; and His
face shone like the sun, and His garments
became as white as light."

MATTHEW 17:2

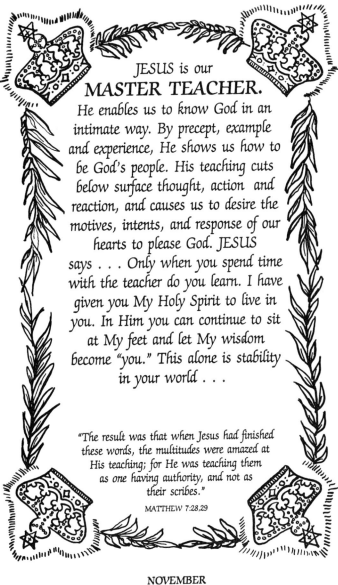

JESUS is our
MASTER TEACHER.

He enables us to know God in an
intimate way. By precept, example
and experience, He shows us how to
be God's people. His teaching cuts
below surface thought, action and
reaction, and causes us to desire the
motives, intents, and response of our
hearts to please God. JESUS
says . . . Only when you spend time
with the teacher do you learn. I have
given you My Holy Spirit to live in
you. In Him you can continue to sit
at My feet and let My wisdom
become "you." This alone is stability
in your world . . .

"The result was that when Jesus had finished
these words, the multitudes were amazed at
His teaching; for He was teaching them
as one having authority, and not as
their scribes."

MATTHEW 7:28,29

JESUS is the
TESTATOR. He is the perfect One
sent by God to make a will which gives
all the promises of God as the rich
inheritance to any who would believe in
Him. His death released God's provision
so that we can begin now to enjoy being
God's adopted children. JESUS says . . .
All I have given you, made possible by
My death and resurrection, have a string
attached. All I have given you—time,
talents, money, spiritual gifts—are to be
used at My direction, in My way, in My
timing for the purpose of bringing all who
will come into My family . . .

"How much more shall the blood of Christ, who
through the eternal Spirit offered himself without
spot to God, purge your conscience from dead
works to serve the living God? . . . For
where a testament is there must also of
necessity be the death of the testator."

HEBREWS 9:14,16 KJV

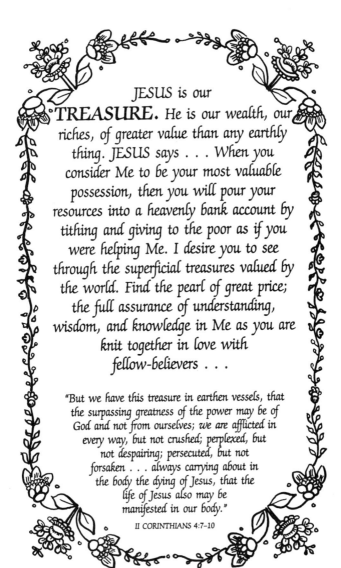

JESUS is our **TREASURE.** He is our wealth, our riches, of greater value than any earthly thing. JESUS says . . . When you consider Me to be your most valuable possession, then you will pour your resources into a heavenly bank account by tithing and giving to the poor as if you were helping Me. I desire you to see through the superficial treasures valued by the world. Find the pearl of great price; the full assurance of understanding, wisdom, and knowledge in Me as you are knit together in love with fellow-believers . . .

"But we have this treasure in earthen vessels, that the surpassing greatness of the power may be of God and not from ourselves; we are afflicted in every way, but not crushed; perplexed, but not despairing; persecuted, but not forsaken . . . always carrying about in the body the dying of Jesus, that the life of Jesus also may be manifested in our body."

II CORINTHIANS 4:7–10

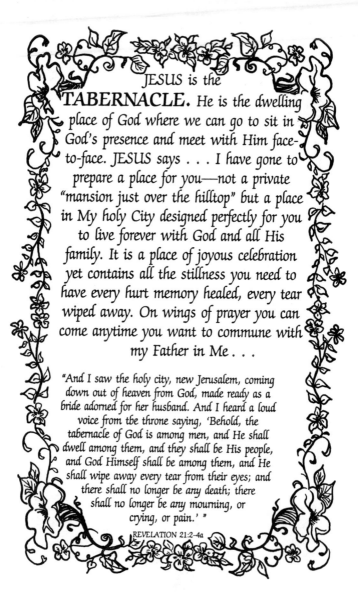

JESUS is the **TABERNACLE.** He is the dwelling place of God where we can go to sit in God's presence and meet with Him face-to-face. JESUS says . . . I have gone to prepare a place for you—not a private "mansion just over the hilltop" but a place in My holy City designed perfectly for you to live forever with God and all His family. It is a place of joyous celebration yet contains all the stillness you need to have every hurt memory healed, every tear wiped away. On wings of prayer you can come anytime you want to commune with my Father in Me . . .

"And I saw the holy city, new Jerusalem, coming down out of heaven from God, made ready as a bride adorned for her husband. And I heard a loud voice from the throne saying, 'Behold, the tabernacle of God is among men, and He shall dwell among them, and they shall be His people, and God Himself shall be among them, and He shall wipe away every tear from their eyes; and there shall no longer be any death; there shall no longer be any mourning, or crying, or pain.' "

REVELATION 21:2–4a

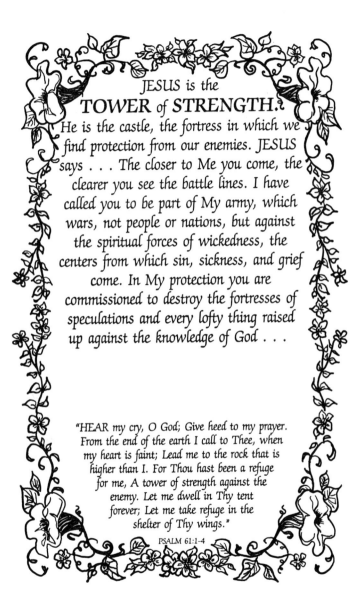

JESUS is the
TOWER of STRENGTH.

He is the castle, the fortress in which we find protection from our enemies. JESUS says . . . The closer to Me you come, the clearer you see the battle lines. I have called you to be part of My army, which wars, not people or nations, but against the spiritual forces of wickedness, the centers from which sin, sickness, and grief come. In My protection you are commissioned to destroy the fortresses of speculations and every lofty thing raised up against the knowledge of God . . .

"HEAR my cry, O God; Give heed to my prayer.
From the end of the earth I call to Thee, when
my heart is faint; Lead me to the rock that is
higher than I. For Thou hast been a refuge
for me, A tower of strength against the
enemy. Let me dwell in Thy tent
forever; Let me take refuge in the
shelter of Thy wings."

PSALM 61:1-4

JESUS is the
TRUTH. He is reality in its essence.
He is the standard for what man is made
to be in relation to God. In Him both
God and man are represented faithfully.
JESUS says . . . Truth involves body,
mind, and spirit. You cannot know Me or
yourself with intellect only—to attempt
this is pride, a miniature Babel. Humble
yourself by coming in through the narrow
gate of belief that I am who I claim to
be. Then wisdom and knowledge will
open to you as a loving gift from
God . . .

"Jesus said to him, 'I am the way, and the truth,
and the life; no one comes to the Father, but
through Me.'"
JOHN 14:6

JESUS is

TRUE. He is steadfast, loyal, faithful, honest, just. He represents God perfectly to us. Every word He spoke and every word He speaks in the quiet of our hearts is consistent with God's Word to Moses and the prophets. JESUS says . . . Earnestly desire to prophesy. Sit at My feet; let Me speak to you, feed you daily through My Word. There is a famine in the land. People are being glutted with words which neither satisfy nor nourish. I want you to hear My word clearly so that you, My disciple, can feed those around you with the little loaf I give you . . .

"... behold, a white horse, and He who sat upon it *is* called Faithful and True; and in righteousness He judges and wages war. And His eyes are a flame of fire, and upon His head are many diadems; and He has a name written upon *Him* which no one knows except Himself. And *He is* clothed with a robe dipped in blood; and His name is called The Word of God."

REVELATION 19:116-13

JESUS is
TENDER. For us He left His preeminence in heaven and took on the fragile, physically weak form of a baby. As He grew, He used supernatural power only as directed by God and to illustrate to His followers what God wants to do through those who believe. Jesus was unashamed of the deep emotions of love and compassion which people's sickness or grief aroused in Him. JESUS says . . . When My Spirit of tenderness is in you, you will not be afraid of what others might think of you. You will weep, groan with those who suffer. You will search My Word till you are able to make a sacrifice of yourself and of praise and see My healing . . .

"For He grew up before Him like a tender shoot, And like a root out of parched ground; He has no stately form or majesty That we should look upon Him . . . Surely our griefs He Himself bore, And our sorrows He carried . . . He was pierced through for our trangressions, He was crushed for our iniquities . . . by His scourging we are healed."

ISAIAH 53:2a,4a,5

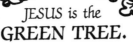

JESUS is the
GREEN TREE.
He is the branch of
Israel which contains life, hope, and
usefulness for God. If we continue to stay
in Him, we have His life coursing
through us. When we choose our own
way, we become worthless as a dry tree,
good only for burning. JESUS says . . .
Tears which do not lead to repentance
have no value. I do not need pity, for in
My choice of the cross there is
resurrection life. If you choose My way
there will be a cross and also abundant
life . . .

"But Jesus turning to them said, 'Daughters of
Jerusalem, stop weeping for Me, but weep for yourselves
and for your children . . . for if they do these things in
the green tree, what will happen in the dry?' "

LUKE 23:28,31

JESUS is
UNSEARCHABLE.

It is impossible for us to explore or find out all of the riches which God has given us in Christ Jesus. JESUS says . . . Let Me daily guide you in your search for My riches. I will lead you into spiritual uncharted waters, virgin forests, and untracked space. Saints who have gone before are cheering for you. My riches are like manna, though. What is found each day must be eaten and become part of you or be given away. My riches are your necessary tools for overcoming the force of evil in the world you explore . . .

"Unto me, who am less than the least of all saints, is this grace given, that I should preach among the Gentiles . . . the unsearchable riches of Christ; And to make all men see what is the fellowship of the mystery, which from the beginning of the world hath been hid in God, who created all things by Jesus Christ: To the intent that now unto the principalities and powers in heavenly places might be known by the church the manifold wisdom of God."

EPHESIANS 3:8–10 KJV

JESUS is the
UNITER. In Him Jew, Arab, and
Gentile, black and white, old and young,
rich and poor, male and female, whether
in Communist, secular humanist or
dictatorial government structures, with all
the distinctiveness God has given them,
come together as equally important and
necessary for wholeness and harmony in
the Body of Jesus. He says . . . Be open
to see Me in all who lift up My name.
As you wrap arms of acceptance around
someone who is different from you, you
will know more fully that My arms hold
you and long to include everyone . . .

"And He gave some as apostles, and some as
prophets, and some as evangelists, and some as
pastors and teachers, for the equipping of the
saints for the work of service, to the building
up of the body of Christ; until we all
attain to the unity of the faith, and of
the knowledge of the Son of God, to
a mature man, to the measure of
the stature which belongs . . .
to the fulness of Christ."

EPHESIANS 4:11–13

JESUS is the
UPHOLDER. He carries us, bears
us up, supports us, endures dangers that
we might be kept close to His heart.
JESUS says . . . The very One who
created you has never left you. The One
who holds all things together holds you
with tenderness. Rest in Me today. Let
My Word surround you, soak into your
soul and enable you to sail with lightness
through life's storms with Me at the
helm . . .

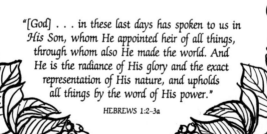

"[God] . . . in these last days has spoken to us in
His Son, whom He appointed heir of all things,
through whom also He made the world. And
He is the radiance of His glory and the exact
representation of His nature, and upholds
all things by the word of His power."

HEBREWS 1:2–3a

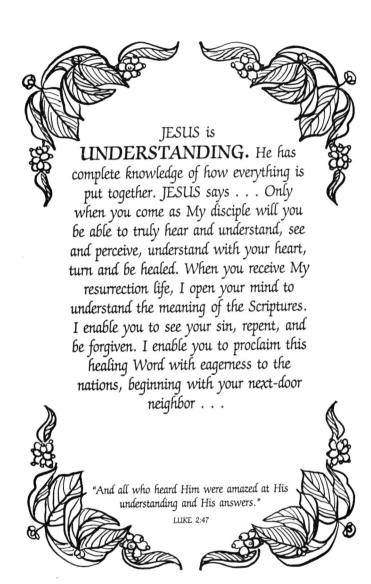

JESUS is
UNDERSTANDING. He has complete knowledge of how everything is put together. JESUS says . . . Only when you come as My disciple will you be able to truly hear and understand, see and perceive, understand with your heart, turn and be healed. When you receive My resurrection life, I open your mind to understand the meaning of the Scriptures. I enable you to see your sin, repent, and be forgiven. I enable you to proclaim this healing Word with eagerness to the nations, beginning with your next-door neighbor . . .

"And all who heard Him were amazed at His understanding and His answers."

LUKE 2:47

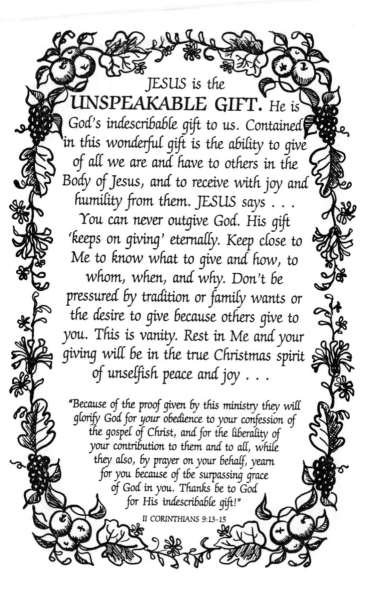

JESUS is the **UNSPEAKABLE GIFT.** He is God's indescribable gift to us. Contained in this wonderful gift is the ability to give of all we are and have to others in the Body of Jesus, and to receive with joy and humility from them. JESUS says . . .

You can never outgive God. His gift 'keeps on giving' eternally. Keep close to Me to know what to give and how, to whom, when, and why. Don't be pressured by tradition or family wants or the desire to give because others give to you. This is vanity. Rest in Me and your giving will be in the true Christmas spirit of unselfish peace and joy . . .

"Because of the proof given by this ministry they will glorify God for your obedience to your confession of the gospel of Christ, and for the liberality of your contribution to them and to all, while they also, by prayer on your behalf, yearn for you because of the surpassing grace of God in you. Thanks be to God for His indescribable gift!"

II CORINTHIANS 9:13–15

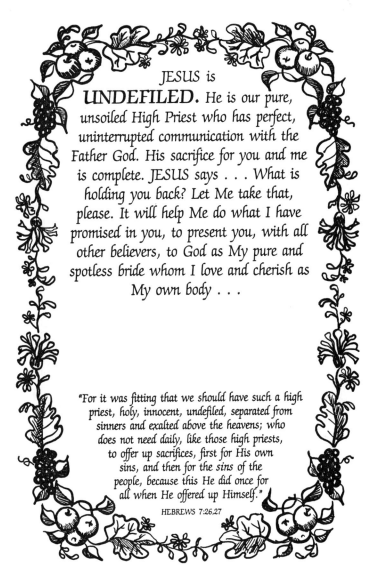

JESUS is

UNDEFILED. He is our pure, unsoiled High Priest who has perfect, uninterrupted communication with the Father God. His sacrifice for you and me is complete. JESUS says . . . What is holding you back? Let Me take that, please. It will help Me do what I have promised in you, to present you, with all other believers, to God as My pure and spotless bride whom I love and cherish as My own body . . .

"For it was fitting that we should have such a high priest, holy, innocent, undefiled, separated from sinners and exalted above the heavens; who does not need daily, like those high priests, to offer up sacrifices, first for His own sins, and then for the sins of the people, because this He did once for all when He offered up Himself."

HEBREWS 7:26,27

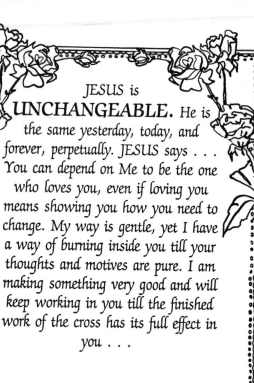

JESUS is
UNCHANGEABLE. He is
the same yesterday, today, and
forever, perpetually. JESUS says . . .
You can depend on Me to be the one
who loves you, even if loving you
means showing you how you need to
change. My way is gentle, yet I have
a way of burning inside you till your
thoughts and motives are pure. I am
making something very good and will
keep working in you till the finished
work of the cross has its full effect in
you . . .

"And they truly were many priests, because
they were not suffered to continue by reason
of death: But this man, because he
continueth ever, hath an unchangeable
priesthood."

HEBREWS 7:23–24 KJV

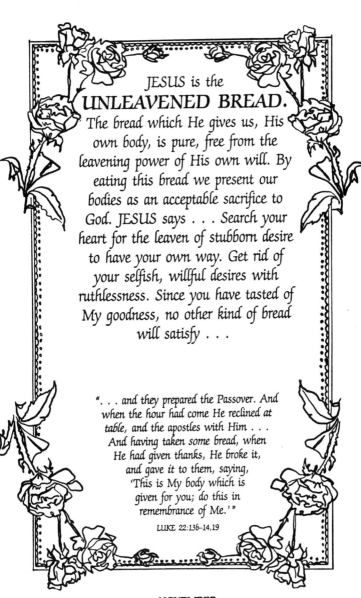

JESUS is the
UNLEAVENED BREAD.
The bread which He gives us, His own body, is pure, free from the leavening power of His own will. By eating this bread we present our bodies as an acceptable sacrifice to God. JESUS says . . . Search your heart for the leaven of stubborn desire to have your own way. Get rid of your selfish, willful desires with ruthlessness. Since you have tasted of My goodness, no other kind of bread will satisfy . . .

" . . . and they prepared the Passover. And when the hour had come He reclined at table, and the apostles with Him . . . And having taken some bread, when He had given thanks, He broke it, and gave it to them, saying, 'This is My body which is given for you; do this in remembrance of Me.' "

LUKE 22:13b–14,19

JESUS has all things **UNDER** His feet. The resurrected Jesus is seated in heavenly places beside God the Father, "far above all rule and authority and power and dominion, and every name that is named, not only in this age, but also in the one to come" (Ephesians 1:21). JESUS says . . . Come, sit with Me. See through, from My perspective, your circumstances and Satan's powers. Do this as an exercise of your will to put off discouragement, petty feelings and doubts. From where we sit there is a joyful solution to your situation and the world's . . .

"And He put all things in subjection under His feet, and gave Him as head over all things to the church, which is His body, the fulness of Him who fills all in all."

EPHESIANS 1:22,23

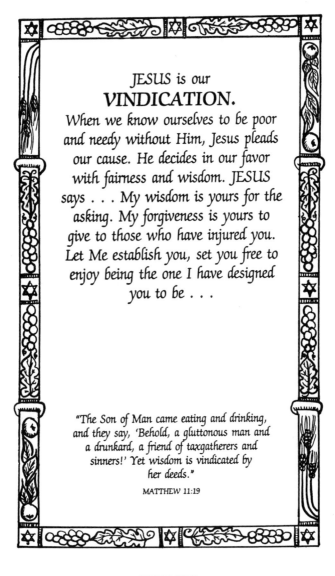

JESUS is our
VINDICATION.
When we know ourselves to be poor
and needy without Him, Jesus pleads
our cause. He decides in our favor
with fairness and wisdom. JESUS
says . . . My wisdom is yours for the
asking. My forgiveness is yours to
give to those who have injured you.
Let Me establish you, set you free to
enjoy being the one I have designed
you to be . . .

"The Son of Man came eating and drinking,
and they say, 'Behold, a gluttonous man and
a drunkard, a friend of taxgatherers and
sinners!' Yet wisdom is vindicated by
her deeds."

MATTHEW 11:19

JESUS is the
TRUE VINE. He is the
productive shoot from the vine of
Israel which produces the fruit of
love, joy, peace, and faith. We must
stay intimately bound to Him for life
abundant. JESUS says . . . From the
tiny seeds of My Spirit within you
grows nourishing, delicious fruit.
Offer this fruit as gifts from Me to
those around you. Seeds from your
contentment, peace, and love will be
planted and spring up in unexpected
places. My joy will heal the hurt
which comes when your living
unproductive branches are cut off by
the Father . . .

"I AM the true vine, and My Father is the
vinedresser. Every branch in Me that does
not bear fruit, He takes away; and every
branch that bears fruit, He prunes it,
that it may bear more fruit."

JOHN 15:1-2

JESUS is the
VIRGIN'S SON.

The miraculous birth of Jesus was prophesied hundreds of years before by Isaiah. A young woman who had never had sexual relations with a man would bear a son whose Father is God. JESUS says . . . I came into the world at My Father's bidding, completely helpless. It pleased God for Me to experience as a human all the uncertainties of life, as well as the warmth of a God-fearing mother. Mary is a sign of what a human can be—willing and obedient to God's way and filled with the Presence of God . . .

"Therefore the Lord Himself will give you a sign: Behold, a virgin will be with child and bear a son, and she will call His name Immanuel."

ISAIAH 7:14

JESUS is the
VINE. He is the trunk which is the channel to the branches of all that is necessary for a productive, fruitful life. JESUS says . . . Stay close to Me. All through the day, stay close to Me. As you live in Me, My vitality, energy, and strength will pour through you. The love, joy, peace, patience, goodness, kindness, faithfulness, gentleness, and self-control you produce is our gift to those around you. Many seeds of like kind are in each of those fruits you give away so that the earth may be replenished . . .

"I am the vine, you are the branches; he who abides in Me, and I in him, he bears much fruit; for apart from Me you can do nothing."

JOHN 15:5

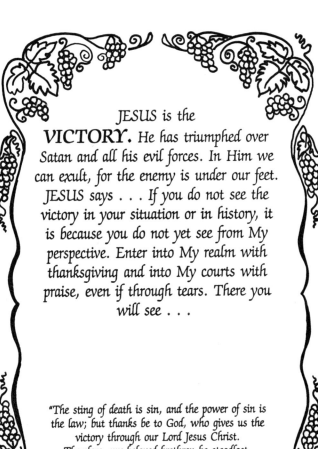

JESUS is the **VICTORY.** He has triumphed over Satan and all his evil forces. In Him we can exult, for the enemy is under our feet. JESUS says . . . If you do not see the victory in your situation or in history, it is because you do not yet see from My perspective. Enter into My realm with thanksgiving and into My courts with praise, even if through tears. There you will see . . .

"The sting of death is sin, and the power of sin is the law; but thanks be to God, who gives us the victory through our Lord Jesus Christ. Therefore, my beloved brethren be steadfast, immovable, always abounding in the work of the Lord, knowing that your toil is not *in* vain in the Lord."

I CORINTHIANS 15:56–58

JESUS is the
VOICE of **GOD.** All who know
Jesus recognize His voice. In
Revelation it thunders like the sound
of many waters. In John it is the
voice of a gentle Shepherd or loving
Bridegroom. If we listen for His
voice, we will hear it. JESUS
says . . . Tune out, turn off all the
artificial, mechanized voices which
surround you. Focus on My voice. I
am speaking to you words of life . . .

"You yourselves, bear me witness, that I said,
'I am not the Christ,' but, 'I have been sent
before Him.' He who has the bride is the
bridegroom; but the friend of the
bridegroom, who stands and hears
him, rejoices greatly because of
the bridegroom's voice. And so
this joy of mine has been
made full. He must
increase, but I must
decrease."

JOHN 3:28–30

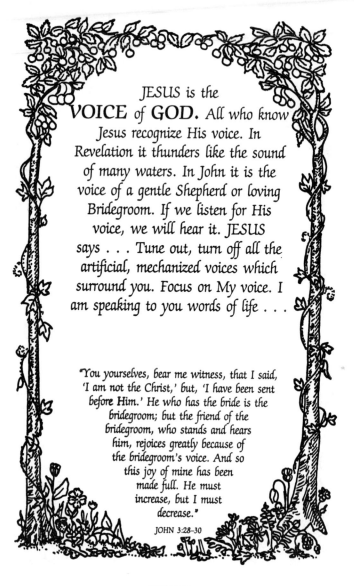

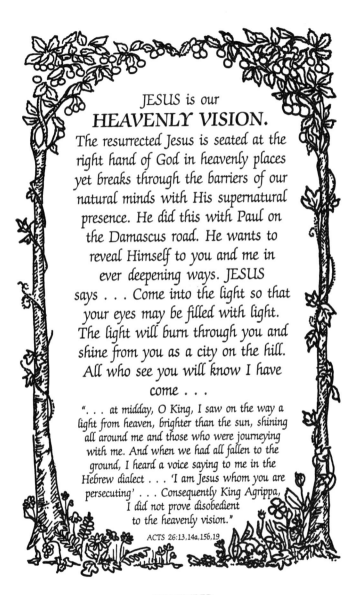

JESUS is our
HEAVENLY VISION.

The resurrected Jesus is seated at the right hand of God in heavenly places yet breaks through the barriers of our natural minds with His supernatural presence. He did this with Paul on the Damascus road. He wants to reveal Himself to you and me in ever deepening ways. JESUS says . . . Come into the light so that your eyes may be filled with light. The light will burn through you and shine from you as a city on the hill. All who see you will know I have come . . .

" . . . at midday, O King, I saw on the way a light from heaven, brighter than the sun, shining all around me and those who were journeying with me. And when we had all fallen to the ground, I heard a voice saying to me in the Hebrew dialect . . . 'I am Jesus whom you are persecuting' . . . Consequently King Agrippa, I did not prove disobedient to the heavenly vision."

ACTS 26:13,14a,15b,19

JESUS is the
VEIL. His body is the Temple of the
Living God. His flesh is the veil into the
holy of holies where the Shekinah, the
glory of God rests. On the cross, this veil
was torn and opened the door for all who
believe to enter into this sacred place to
commune with God face-to-face. JESUS
says . . . Enter in. Earnestly desire to
enter in. There is much the Father and I
would share with you, but you must
enter in . . .

"Since therefore, brethren, we have confidence to enter
the holy place by the blood of Jesus, by a new and
living way which He inaugurated for us
through the veil, that is, His flesh, and since
we have a great priest over the house of
God Let us draw near with a sincere
heart in full assurance of faith,
having our hearts sprinkled clean
from an evil conscience and
our bodies washed with
pure water."

HEBREWS 10:19–22

JESUS is the
WORKER. By doing exactly what
His Father, God, instructed Him, Jesus
was able to do many marvelous miracles
where there was an atmosphere of
expectancy. JESUS says . . . By
immersing yourself in My WORD as if it
were written for you, by worshiping with
faith-filled people, you increase the level of
your own faith. I want you to believe
that through you, as well as through men
and women of God through the ages,
greater things than I did are possible. You
are My fellow-workers . . .

"Believe Me that I am in the Father, and the Father
in Me; otherwise believe on account of the works
themselves. Truly, truly, I say to you, he who
believes in Me, the works that I do shall he
do also; and greater works than these
shall he do; because I go to the
Father."

JOHN 14:11,12

JESUS is the
WORD. He is God's preexistent,
personal, creative, illuminating, revealing,
incarnate, superior, powerful, fulfilled,
Messianic Word. He contains both the
meaning of God's thoughts and His
spoken Word, His reason and that
reason's expression, which is definite,
ordered, and complete. JESUS says . . .
Let My Word speak to your heart to
create in you something new, something
fresh, clean, and beautiful. As you soak in
My Word daily, I become part of you and
you of Me so that we are One . . .

"In the beginning was the Word, and the Word was
with God, and the Word was God. He was in the
beginning with God. All things came into being
through Him; and apart from Him nothing
came into being that has come into being.
In Him was life; and the life was the
light of men."

JOHN 1:1-4

JESUS is
WORTHY. He is deserving of the highest praise from people of every tribe and tongue and nation. Blessing, honor, glory, and dominion are due Him from every created thing whether in heaven or in the earth. JESUS says . . . When you praise Me, you praise the Father and the Holy Spirit, for We are one. What is worthy of praise? Think about this. Beyond the initial creative act was the giving of the Creator Himself for the created—you. All praise is due Me, because I gave all for you. By praising Me you get in touch with and grow to be like the very One you admire . . .

"And I looked, and I heard the voice of many angels around the throne and the living creatures and the elders; and the number of them was myriads of myriads, and thousands of thousands, saying with a loud voice, 'Worthy is the Lamb that was slain to receive power and riches and wisdom and might and honor and glory and blessing.'"

REVELATION 5:11–12

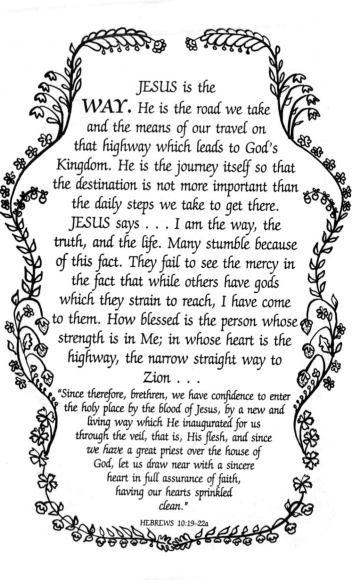

JESUS is the **WAY.** He is the road we take and the means of our travel on that highway which leads to God's Kingdom. He is the journey itself so that the destination is not more important than the daily steps we take to get there.

JESUS says . . . I am the way, the truth, and the life. Many stumble because of this fact. They fail to see the mercy in the fact that while others have gods which they strain to reach, I have come to them. How blessed is the person whose strength is in Me; in whose heart is the highway, the narrow straight way to Zion . . .

"Since therefore, brethren, we have confidence to enter the holy place by the blood of Jesus, by a new and living way which He inaugurated for us through the veil, that is, His flesh, and since we have a great priest over the house of God, let us draw near with a sincere heart in full assurance of faith, having our hearts sprinkled clean."

HEBREWS 10:19–22a

JESUS is the
WATER of **LIFE.**
He is the source of the supply of the
fountain which gushes forth living water,
the essence of life which is in Jesus'
blood. In Him is the possibility of fullest
enjoyment. JESUS says . . . Let the
waters of My life well up in you and flow
out in a never-ending stream. When you
feel dry, speak to the Source and say,
'Spring up, O well.' Through the hard,
rocky places of your life, joy and peace
will tumble forth and cause you to be a
pleasure to be with . . .

"Jesus answered and said to her, 'Everyone who
drinks of this water shall thirst again; but
whoever drinks of the water that I shall give
him shall never thirst; but the water that I
shall give him shall become in him a well
of water springing up to eternal life.'"

JOHN 4:13,14

JESUS is the

NEW WINE. He has made holy the
common drink of His day, juice from
grapes which have been pressed and
squeezed. He told the disciples that the
wine He offers us is His blood. When we
drink it, His blood pours into us. JESUS
says . . . I want to be in you, flow
through you in ever more complete ways.
Drink of the costly wine of My blood. As
you are forgiven, forgive those around you
who press and squeeze you . . .

"And He took a cup and gave thanks, and gave it to
them saying, 'Drink from it, all of you,' for this
is My blood of the covenant, which is to be
shed on behalf of many for forgiveness of
sins.' "

MATTHEW 26:27,28

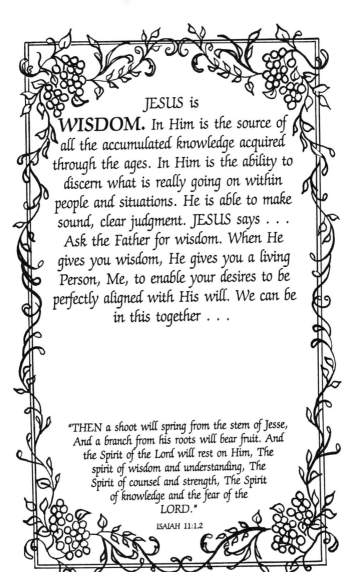

JESUS is

WISDOM. In Him is the source of all the accumulated knowledge acquired through the ages. In Him is the ability to discern what is really going on within people and situations. He is able to make sound, clear judgment. JESUS says . . . Ask the Father for wisdom. When He gives you wisdom, He gives you a living Person, Me, to enable your desires to be perfectly aligned with His will. We can be in this together . . .

"THEN a shoot will spring from the stem of Jesse, And a branch from his roots will bear fruit. And the Spirit of the Lord will rest on Him, The spirit of wisdom and understanding, The Spirit of counsel and strength, The Spirit of knowledge and the fear of the LORD."

ISAIAH 11:1,2

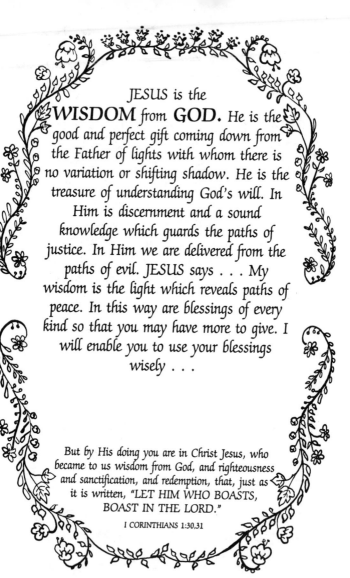

JESUS is the **WISDOM** from **GOD.** He is the good and perfect gift coming down from the Father of lights with whom there is no variation or shifting shadow. He is the treasure of understanding God's will. In Him is discernment and a sound knowledge which guards the paths of justice. In Him we are delivered from the paths of evil. JESUS says . . . My wisdom is the light which reveals paths of peace. In this way are blessings of every kind so that you may have more to give. I will enable you to use your blessings wisely . . .

But by His doing you are in Christ Jesus, who became to us wisdom from God, and righteousness and sanctification, and redemption, that, just as it is written, "LET HIM WHO BOASTS, BOAST IN THE LORD."

I CORINTHIANS 1:30,31

JESUS is
WONDERFUL.

He is full of wonders: miracles, marvels, exciting and astonishing things are done by Him. JESUS says . . . You are part of My Body. Today expect My compassion to flow through you so that wonderful things will happen. If you expect a miracle you will thank Me, praise Me, glorify My name now. Each miracle you see and praise Me for is just a tiny taste of what I am accomplishing. As Isaiah said, there will be no end to the increase of My government or of peace . . .

"For a child will be born to us, a son will be given to us; And the government will rest on His shoulders; And His Name will be called Wonderful Counselor, Mighty God, Eternal Father, Prince of Peace."

ISAIAH 9:6

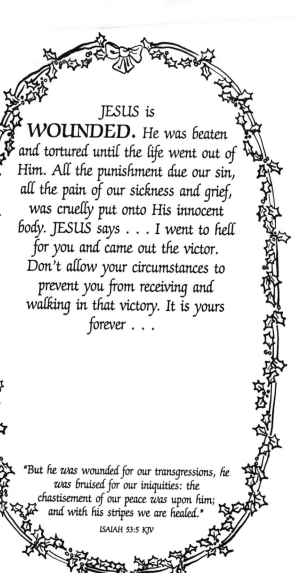

JESUS is
WOUNDED. He was beaten
and tortured until the life went out of
Him. All the punishment due our sin,
all the pain of our sickness and grief,
was cruelly put onto His innocent
body. JESUS says . . . I went to hell
for you and came out the victor.
Don't allow your circumstances to
prevent you from receiving and
walking in that victory. It is yours
forever . . .

"But he *was* wounded for our transgressions, he
was bruised for our iniquities: the
chastisement of our peace *was* upon him;
and with his stripes we are healed."

ISAIAH 53:5 KJV

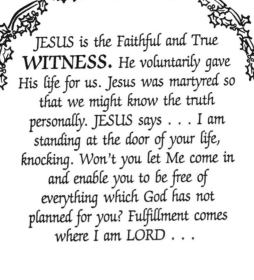

JESUS is the Faithful and True **WITNESS.** He voluntarily gave His life for us. Jesus was martyred so that we might know the truth personally. JESUS says . . . I am standing at the door of your life, knocking. Won't you let Me come in and enable you to be free of everything which God has not planned for you? Fulfillment comes where I am LORD . . .

". . . The Amen, the faithful and true Witness, the Beginning of the creation of God, says this . . . I advise you to buy from Me gold refined by fire, that you may become rich, and white garments, that you may clothe yourself . . . and eyesalve to anoint your eyes, that you may see. Those whom I love, I reprove and discipline; be zealous, therefore, and repent."

REVELATION 3:14b,18–19

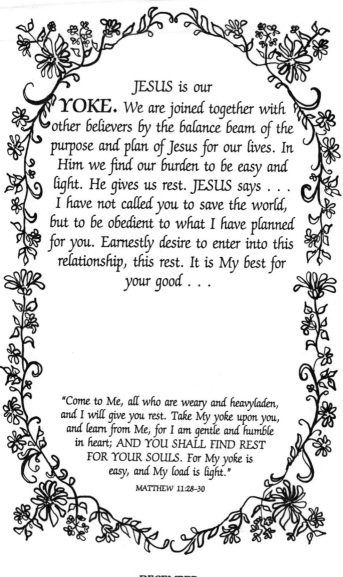

JESUS is our
YOKE. We are joined together with
other believers by the balance beam of the
purpose and plan of Jesus for our lives. In
Him we find our burden to be easy and
light. He gives us rest. JESUS says . . .
I have not called you to save the world,
but to be obedient to what I have planned
for you. Earnestly desire to enter into this
relationship, this rest. It is My best for
your good . . .

"Come to Me, all who are weary and heavyladen,
and I will give you rest. Take My yoke upon you,
and learn from Me, for I am gentle and humble
in heart; AND YOU SHALL FIND REST
FOR YOUR SOULS. For My yoke is
easy, and My load is light."

MATTHEW 11:28–30

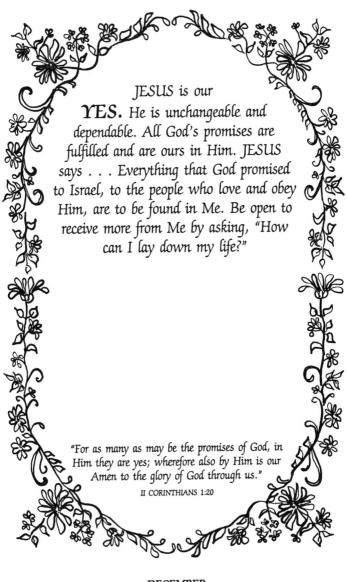

JESUS is our **YES.** He is unchangeable and dependable. All God's promises are fulfilled and are ours in Him. JESUS says . . . Everything that God promised to Israel, to the people who love and obey Him, are to be found in Me. Be open to receive more from Me by asking, "How can I lay down my life?"

"For as many as may be the promises of God, in Him they are yes; wherefore also by Him is our Amen to the glory of God through us."

II CORINTHIANS 1:20

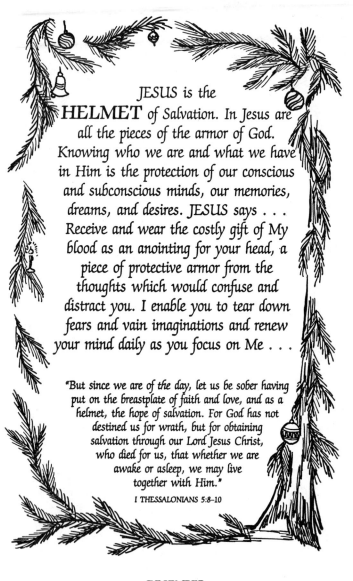

JESUS is the
HELMET of Salvation. In Jesus are
all the pieces of the armor of God.
Knowing who we are and what we have
in Him is the protection of our conscious
and subconscious minds, our memories,
dreams, and desires. JESUS says . . .
Receive and wear the costly gift of My
blood as an anointing for your head, a
piece of protective armor from the
thoughts which would confuse and
distract you. I enable you to tear down
fears and vain imaginations and renew
your mind daily as you focus on Me . . .

"But since we are of the day, let us be sober having
put on the breastplate of faith and love, and as a
helmet, the hope of salvation. For God has not
destined us for wrath, but for obtaining
salvation through our Lord Jesus Christ,
who died for us, that whether we are
awake or asleep, we may live
together with Him."

I THESSALONIANS 5:8–10

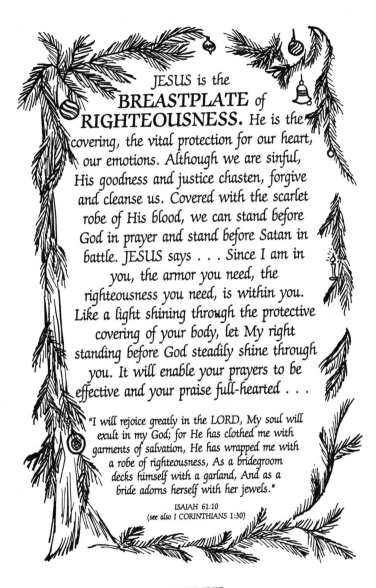

JESUS is the **BREASTPLATE** of **RIGHTEOUSNESS.** He is the covering, the vital protection for our heart, our emotions. Although we are sinful, His goodness and justice chasten, forgive and cleanse us. Covered with the scarlet robe of His blood, we can stand before God in prayer and stand before Satan in battle. JESUS says . . . Since I am in you, the armor you need, the righteousness you need, is within you. Like a light shining through the protective covering of your body, let My right standing before God steadily shine through you. It will enable your prayers to be effective and your praise full-hearted . . .

"I will rejoice greatly in the LORD, My soul will exult in my God; for He has clothed me with garments of salvation, He has wrapped me with a robe of righteousness, As a bridegroom decks himself with a garland, And as a bride adorns herself with her jewels."

ISAIAH 61:10
(see also I CORINTHIANS 1:30)

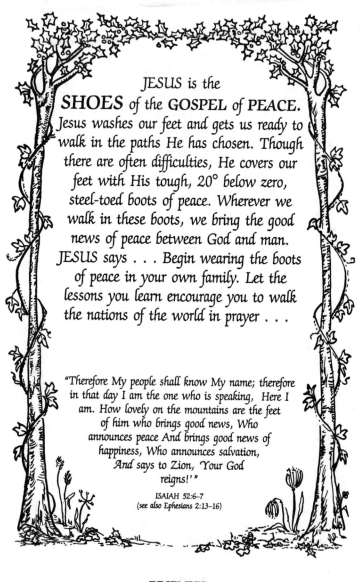

JESUS is the
SHOES of the GOSPEL of PEACE.
Jesus washes our feet and gets us ready to walk in the paths He has chosen. Though there are often difficulties, He covers our feet with His tough, 20° below zero, steel-toed boots of peace. Wherever we walk in these boots, we bring the good news of peace between God and man. JESUS says . . . Begin wearing the boots of peace in your own family. Let the lessons you learn encourage you to walk the nations of the world in prayer . . .

"Therefore My people shall know My name; therefore in that day I am the one who is speaking, Here I am. How lovely on the mountains are the feet of him who brings good news, Who announces peace And brings good news of happiness, Who announces salvation, And says to Zion, 'Your God reigns!'"

ISAIAH 52:6–7
(see also Ephesians 2:13–16)

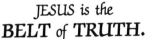

JESUS is the
BELT of TRUTH.

In His fidelity and constancy we are held
secure. Spiritual reality in Jesus protects
the vital parts of His body; we are both
in Him and covered by Him. JESUS
says . . . Wise men have sought to know
the truth which would set them free, yet
are offended by Me. When you submit to
My love encircling you, you will know
the Truth and be glad . . .

*"Jesus said to him, 'I am the way, and the truth,
and the life; no one comes to the Father, but
through Me. If you had known Me, you would
have known My Father also; from now on
you know Him, and have seen Him.'"*

JOHN 14:6,7

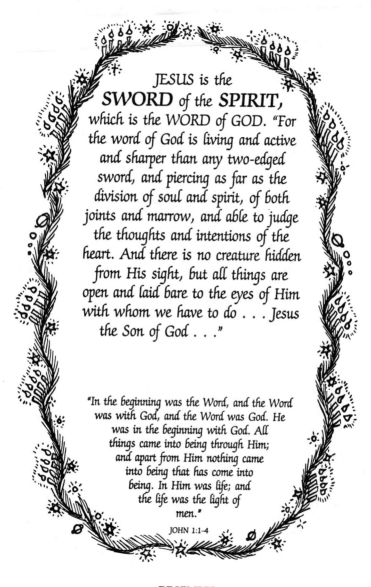

JESUS is the
SWORD of the **SPIRIT,**
which is the WORD of GOD. "For
the word of God is living and active
and sharper than any two-edged
sword, and piercing as far as the
division of soul and spirit, of both
joints and marrow, and able to judge
the thoughts and intentions of the
heart. And there is no creature hidden
from His sight, but all things are
open and laid bare to the eyes of Him
with whom we have to do . . . Jesus
the Son of God . . ."

"In the beginning was the Word, and the Word
was with God, and the Word was God. He
was in the beginning with God. All
things came into being through Him;
and apart from Him nothing came
into being that has come into
being. In Him was life; and
the life was the light of
men."

JOHN 1:1-4

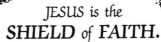

JESUS is the
SHIELD of FAITH.

From head to toe the impenetrable
shield of faith is ours in Jesus to hold
against every fiery missile hurled at us
by the prince of darkness. This shield
is inextricably linked to the Word of
God. ". . . Continue in the things
you have learned and become
convinced of, knowing from whom
you have learned *them*; and that from
childhood you have known the sacred
writings which are able to give you
the wisdom that leads to salvation
through faith which is in Christ
Jesus."

"THEREFORE, since we have so great a cloud
of witnesses surrounding us, let us lay aside
every encumbrance, and the sin which so
easily entangles us, and let us run
with endurance the race that is set
before us, fixing our eyes on
Jesus, the author and perfecter
of faith."

HEBREWS 12:1-2a

THE God of the Old Testament is Jehovah-Jireh, "the Lord will provide" a sacrifice.

Then Abraham raised his eyes and looked, and behold, behind him a ram caught in the thicket by his horns; and Abraham went and took the ram, and offered him up for a burnt offering in the place of his son. And Abraham called the name of that place The LORD Will Provide, as it is said to this day, "In the mount of the LORD it will be provided."

GENESIS 22:13–14

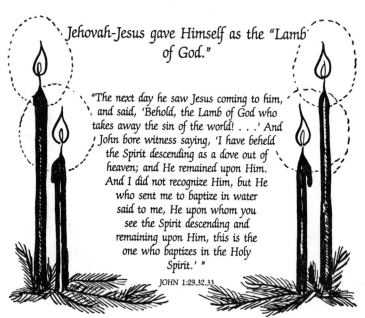

Jehovah-Jesus gave Himself as the "Lamb of God."

"The next day he saw Jesus coming to him, and said, 'Behold, the Lamb of God who takes away the sin of the world! . . .' And John bore witness saying, 'I have beheld the Spirit descending as a dove out of heaven; and He remained upon Him. And I did not recognize Him, but He who sent me to baptize in water said to me, He upon whom you see the Spirit descending and remaining upon Him, this is the one who baptizes in the Holy Spirit.' "

JOHN 1:29,32,33

The God of the Old Testament is Jehovah-Rapha, "I am the Lord that Healeth thee."

"And He said, 'If you will give earnest heed to the voice of the LORD your God, and do what is right in His sight and give ear to His commandments, and keep all His statutes, I will put none of the diseases on you which I have put on the Egyptians; for I, the LORD, am your healer.'"

EXODUS 15:26

Jehovah-Jesus is the Healer.

"And when evening had come, they brought to Him many who were demon-possessed; and He cast out the spirits with a word, and healed all who were ill in order that what was spoken through Isaiah the prophet might be fulfilled, saying, 'HE HIMSELF TOOK OUR INFIRMITIES, AND CARRIED AWAY OUR DISEASES.'"

MATTHEW 8:16,17

יְהֹוָה רָפָא

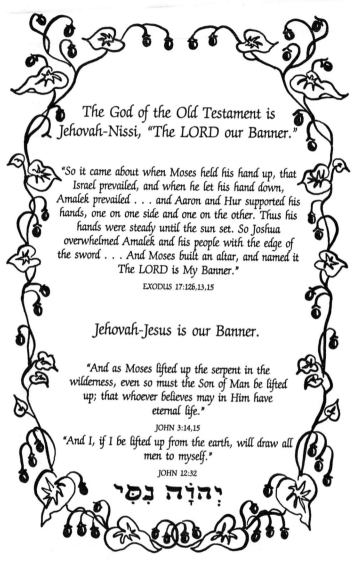

The God of the Old Testament is
Jehovah-Nissi, "The LORD our Banner."

"So it came about when Moses held his hand up, that
Israel prevailed, and when he let his hand down,
Amalek prevailed . . . and Aaron and Hur supported his
hands, one on one side and one on the other. Thus his
hands were steady until the sun set. So Joshua
overwhelmed Amalek and his people with the edge of
the sword . . . And Moses built an altar, and named it
The LORD is My Banner."

EXODUS 17:12b,13,15

Jehovah-Jesus is our Banner.

"And as Moses lifted up the serpent in the
wilderness, even so must the Son of Man be lifted
up; that whoever believes may in Him have
eternal life."

JOHN 3:14,15

"And I, if I be lifted up from the earth, will draw all
men to myself."

JOHN 12:32

יְהֹוָה נִסִּי

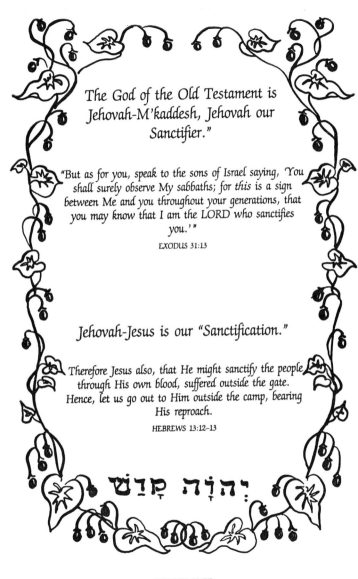

The God of the Old Testament is
Jehovah-M'kaddesh, Jehovah our
Sanctifier."

"But as for you, speak to the sons of Israel saying, 'You
shall surely observe My sabbaths; for this is a sign
between Me and you throughout your generations, that
you may know that I am the LORD who sanctifies
you.' "

EXODUS 31:13

Jehovah-Jesus is our "Sanctification."

Therefore Jesus also, that He might sanctify the people
through His own blood, suffered outside the gate.
Hence, let us go out to Him outside the camp, bearing
His reproach.

HEBREWS 13:12–13

יְהֹוָה קָדֹשׁ

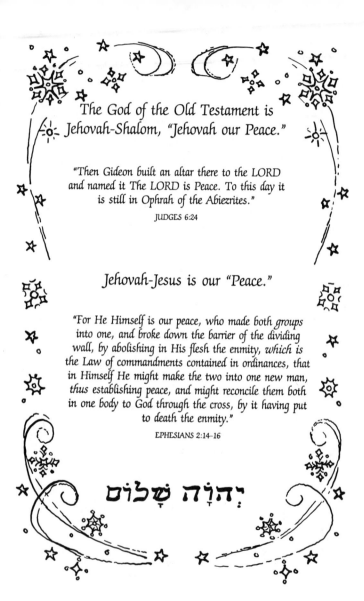

The God of the Old Testament is
Jehovah-Shalom, "Jehovah our Peace."

"Then Gideon built an altar there to the LORD
and named it The LORD is Peace. To this day it
is still in Ophrah of the Abiezrites."

JUDGES 6:24

Jehovah-Jesus is our "Peace."

"For He Himself is our peace, who made both groups
into one, and broke down the barrier of the dividing
wall, by abolishing in His flesh the enmity, which is
the Law of commandments contained in ordinances, that
in Himself He might make the two into one new man,
thus establishing peace, and might reconcile them both
in one body to God through the cross, by it having put
to death the enmity."

EPHESIANS 2:14–16

יְהוָה שָׁלוֹם

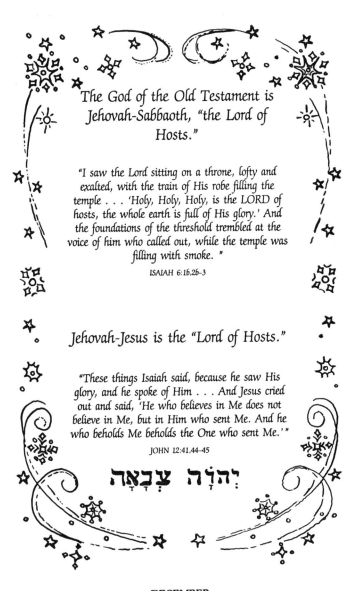

The God of the Old Testament is Jehovah-Sabbaoth, "the Lord of Hosts."

"I saw the Lord sitting on a throne, lofty and exalted, with the train of His robe filling the temple . . . 'Holy, Holy, Holy, is the LORD of hosts, the whole earth is full of His glory.' And the foundations of the threshold trembled at the voice of him who called out, while the temple was filling with smoke. "

ISAIAH 6:1b,2b–3

Jehovah-Jesus is the "Lord of Hosts."

"These things Isaiah said, because he saw His glory, and he spoke of Him . . . And Jesus cried out and said, 'He who believes in Me does not believe in Me, but in Him who sent Me. And he who beholds Me beholds the One who sent Me.'"

JOHN 12:41,44–45

יְהוָה צְבָאָה

The God of the Old Testament is
Jehovah-Elyon, "The Lord Most
High."

"I will give thanks to the LORD according to His
righteousness, And will sing praise to the name of
the LORD Most High."

PSALM 7:17

Jehovah-Jesus is the "Most High."

"GOD, after He spoke long ago to the fathers in
the prophets in many portions and in many ways,
in these last days has spoken to us in *His* Son,
whom He appointed heir of all things, through
whom also He made the world. And He is the
radiance of His glory and the exact representation
of His nature, and upholds all things by the word
of His power. When He had made purification of
sins, He sat down at the right hand of the
Majesty on high; having become as much better
than the angels, as He has inherited a more
excellent name than they."

HEBREWS 1:1-4

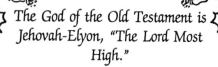

The God of the Old Testament is
Jehovah-Raah, Jehovah my
"Shepherd."

"THE LORD is my shepherd, I shall not want.
He makes me lie down in green pastures; He leads
me beside quiet waters. He restores my soul; He
guides me in the paths of righteousness For His
name's sake."

PSALM 23:1–3

Jehovah-Jesus is our "Shepherd."

"I am the good shepherd; the good shepherd lays
down His life for the sheep . . . I am the good
shepherd; and I know My own, and My own
know Me, even as the Father knows Me and I
know the Father; and I lay down My life for the
sheep. And I have other sheep, which are not of
this fold; I must bring them also, and they shall
hear My voice; and they shall become one flock
with one shepherd."

JOHN 10:11,14–16

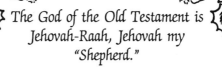

רֹעֶה יְהוָה

The God of the Old Testament is
Jehovah-Tsidkenu, "Jehovah our
Righteousness."

"for the LORD is righteous; He loves
righteousness; The upright will behold His face."

PSALM 11:7

Jehovah-Jesus is our "Righteousness."

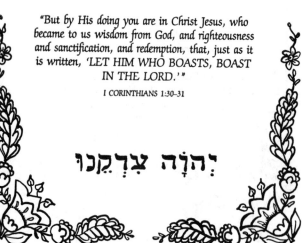

"But by His doing you are in Christ Jesus, who
became to us wisdom from God, and righteousness
and sanctification, and redemption, that, just as it
is written, 'LET HIM WHO BOASTS, BOAST
IN THE LORD.'"

I CORINTHIANS 1:30–31

יְהֹוָה צִדְקֵנוּ

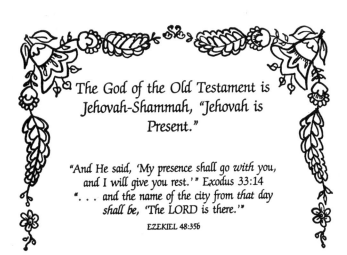

The God of the Old Testament is Jehovah-Shammah, "Jehovah is Present."

"And He said, 'My presence shall go with you, and I will give you rest.'" Exodus 33:14
". . . and the name of the city from that day shall be, 'The LORD is there.'"

EZEKIEL 48:35b

Jehovah-Jesus is Present.

"And JESUS came up and spoke to them, saying, 'All authority has been given to Me in heaven and on earth. Go therefore and make disciples of all the nations, baptizing them in the name of the Father and the Son and the Holy Spirit, teaching them to observe all that I commanded you; and lo, I am with you always, even to the end of the age.'"

MATTHEW 28:18-20

שָׁם יְהֹוָה

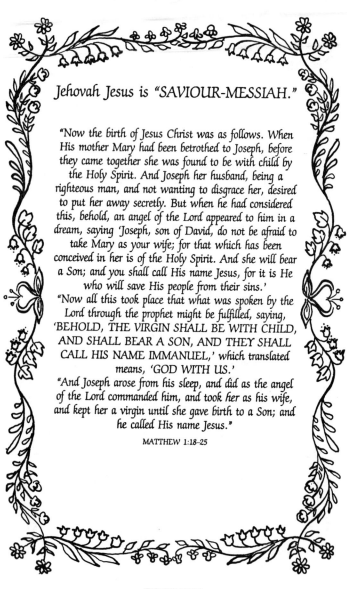

Jehovah Jesus is "SAVIOUR-MESSIAH."

"Now the birth of Jesus Christ was as follows. When His mother Mary had been betrothed to Joseph, before they came together she was found to be with child by the Holy Spirit. And Joseph her husband, being a righteous man, and not wanting to disgrace her, desired to put her away secretly. But when he had considered this, behold, an angel of the Lord appeared to him in a dream, saying 'Joseph, son of David, do not be afraid to take Mary as your wife; for that which has been conceived in her is of the Holy Spirit. And she will bear a Son; and you shall call His name Jesus, for it is He who will save His people from their sins.'

"Now all this took place that what was spoken by the Lord through the prophet might be fulfilled, saying, 'BEHOLD, THE VIRGIN SHALL BE WITH CHILD, AND SHALL BEAR A SON, AND THEY SHALL CALL HIS NAME IMMANUEL,' which translated means, 'GOD WITH US.'

"And Joseph arose from his sleep, and did as the angel of the Lord commanded him, and took her as his wife, and kept her a virgin until she gave birth to a Son; and he called His name Jesus."

MATTHEW 1:18–25